WRITE WITHOUT CRUSHING YOUR SOUL

SUSTAINABLE PUBLISHING AND FREELANCING

ED CYZEWSKI

Write without Crushing Your Soul

Sustainable Publishing and Freelancing

By Ed Cyzewski

You're Invited to Join My Community of Readers
You can get TWO FREE eBooks, first dibs (as well as discounts) on new book releases, and learn about my other books by signing up for my e-newsletter at www.edcyzewski.com.

I also post weekly at www.edcyzewski.com about writing and prayer, and I spend a bit of time each day on Facebook and Twitter. I'd love it if you dropped by to say hello.

ISBN-13:978-1518794667

ISBN-10:1518794661

CONTENTS

ED CYZEWSKI

INTRODUCTION

"When do you find the time to write when you're supposed to spend so much time on marketing?"

"I've always wanted to write a book, but I'm afraid no one will read it."

"After this I finish writing this book, I'm done with commercial publishing."

"I really struggle with comparing my writing work to the success of others."

"How do you keep going as a writer after facing so much rejection?"

"I feel called to write, but I don't think I can or should make a living from it."

Those are just a few of the comments and questions that come up when I talk with current or aspiring authors in person or on social media. We all love to write, and some of us even earn some money from it, but we're all wary of the rejection, comparison, promotion, and uncertain finances that frequently accompany a career in writing. Even worse, some writers invest significant time and money in writing for a particular audience and topic, and after a few years, they run out of ideas, energy, or will to continue. What they once loved becomes a burden. They feel trapped because their writing has become a source of personal identity or income Even if they did start over, they wouldn't know what to work on next. In fact, the pressure of the next book project, blog post, article, marketing task, etc. can wear down even the most talented writers.

We can find true peace and security in our day-to-day lives if we center our lives around God's love that takes root and flourishes in our souls. We know that we are loved and can pursue our work with the assurance of what true acceptance is like, never substituting an audience or editor's acceptance for the security that comes from God's love.

That may sound far-fetched, but you would be surprised to see how many writers are waiting for an editor, agent, or other publishing gatekeeper to validate their work and, by connection, themselves. Others may be anxious wrecks as they wait for a client's feedback, sift through the wreckage of a blog's comment section, or manage the noise coming from social media. Even the writers with a strong sense of personal security and calling to write may deeply struggle to connect with new readers, clients, or important contacts in their networks.

Writing is an intensely personal career. Whether you're marketing a book or writing for your own website, both can feel like extensions of yourself. These works represent your best stories or ideas, and you don't want to cheapen them by promoting them to the hilt even if you're terrified of them being rejected or ignored. By the same token, writing for a publication or business still represents something creative that you've developed. It's not like you're presenting an objective analysis of your company's sales. Your value to clients or your company is on the line with each new website, product manual, or article for publication. I have felt the crush of disappointing my business clients and the elation that comes from delighting my clients. I know what it's like to pour myself into book projects and websites that have sometimes been met with shrugs and other times met with genuine gratitude.

In the midst of the demanding ups and downs of the writing life, there's your soul that can be encouraged and refreshed through your writing or crushed. Your soul is the spiritual part of you, the place where you can meet with God and find security. The writer of the Psalms describes his soul thirsting for the living God. Jesus warned us, "What good is it to gain the whole world and forfeit your soul?"

If you aren't quite sure what to make of your soul, how to find it, or whether it's even worth discussing when there's important writing business to do, I have a suggestion: You'll only be able to figure out the vital importance of your soul if you take the time to find it. I know that may sound like a huge leap of faith to some. The best I can offer is that Jesus tends to have some pretty good ideas that have worked out for me so far. Nurturing and guarding my soul in the midst of the challenges of my writing career has proven revolutionary and life giving for my personal life, work, and spirituality. In addition, it's very possible that most people have so many things piling up on their souls that they wouldn't even know where to begin looking. Your soul may be downcast and weary, and you may not even know there's any other way to live. You may also fear that the challenges of writing professionally, or at least part time, will do further damage to your soul that may be difficult to bear.

Perhaps the question you need to ask right now is this: What do you have to lose right now? Could it be that there's a part of you that has yet to be fully nurtured and released into the world? Even if you don't agree with the religious aspect of your soul as I've been discussing it, perhaps you can take a step toward a more authentic identity and sustainable work life. In the best-case scenario, you could discover what God has placed within you and develop ways to write sustainably without crushing it.

We'll begin with some foundational thoughts about your soul and personal identity. That will include some thoughts on writing sustainably with courage and boundaries. Then the chapters that follow will address more specific topics.

A Foundation for All Writers

I suspect that a broad range of writers will read this book, and therefore I'm going to cover a broad range of professional writing topics. I've limited myself to addressing the types of writing that I've personally worked in since I started writing professionally for businesses in 2003 and then as an author starting in 2008. I've written for websites, small businesses, blogs, newsletters, commercial publishers, and my own independent publishing projects. You could generally break my experience in the writing field into four categories: blogging and websites, book writing and editing, magazines and other publications, and business writing/freelancing. I am writing this with the assumption that those looking for a source of income through writing will also want to explore a creative outlet such as a personal website or book project.

At the same time, I'm assuming that every writer interested in a personal website or book project may also want to know something about writing for businesses, publications, or other freelance opportunities. I'm well aware that readers of this book are on a spectrum, and this book will vary at times from very specific advice about a topic such as book publicity to very general advice about comparing ourselves to others or dealing with adversity as a writer. There may be sections that you'll choose to skip if you're not particularly interested in writing a book or writing for a business.

The most important thing in my view is offering a solid foundation for you as a writer of faith. I want to give you some general advice about what you can personally expect as a blogger, freelancer, or author as well as how you can handle the challenges that come your way. While I trust that any writer could benefit from this book, I want to address the specific challenges that Christians face in the writing profession. I welcome readers with different beliefs to read this book, but there is a foundational assumption that writers will benefit by guarding and nurturing their God-given souls. If you find that preposterous to begin with, you may find this book less than useful.

You can increase your awareness of your soul by removing the burdens that pile up on top of it and inviting God to define who you are and where your writing fits. Writers can guard their souls by frankly facing the challenges of their field, developing strategies that mitigate the negative impact on their souls, and keeping space in their lives for their souls to thrive. Best yet, you'll get a lot more than a pat on the back from Jesus if you care for your soul. You'll discover the single most important priority in all of life: the intense love of God for you that author Brennan Manning describes as God's furious longing for us.

Your soul is where you meet with God, but you can fill that space up with plenty of other things. If God isn't defining who you are, you'll find another source of your identity. As you get caught up in the rigors of writing each day, it will become far more difficult to remain grounded in a sense of your identity and calling if you don't know what it feels like to be centered and grounded. The weight of publicity, criticism, and endless to-do lists can pile up, and we may even begin to despair that there's no way to pursue writing as a career and remain healthy.

We all face different challenges that could crush our souls. Some of us are overcome with crippling insecurity, while others are convinced we're on the brink of writing the next bestseller--I've been guilty of the latter far too often. Some of us are perfectionists who can't stop tweaking a piece of writing, while others are too willing to ship out a really, really rough first draft. Some of us are so desperate for success that we'll flood our friends and family with promotions of our writing, while others can hardly bear the thought of telling anyone other than a spouse or close friend about a book contract.

Having said that, I can't make myself any clearer at the start here: this isn't just a book about writing and soul care within the Christian bubble, merely working with Christians or writing for Christians. The last thing I want to do is create a sub-genre of writing books with the "Christian" descriptor that offer the "Christian alternative" to what already exists in the mainstream. Just writing this book in the first place runs that risk, but I think it's worth taking because the private conversations Christian writers have about writing and publishing can be very, very different from what you'll hear in more mainstream publishing networks, even if the nature of our work, writing things such as books or business copy, is quite similar in substance. Even worse, few Christian writers openly discuss these unique challenges because they think they're alone with these struggles to build a platform, to engage endlessly on social media, to count their numbers constantly, to network with influencers (even in ways that feel cheap and inauthentic), to get invited to bigger events, and to always keep building and selling and growing just to make a living doing something they thought they loved but may not be sure about any more.

Yes, writing and publishing are businesses, but at a certain point writers of faith will face decisions about whether they will guard themselves as creative people of faith or will do whatever it takes to become highly productive workers who jump through all of the hoops in an industry. A few walk this fine line well, but you would be surprised to find out how many bloggers and authors of faith view their writing careers as a mixed blessing at times. For instance, if you create your own schedule and boundaries as a freelance writer, your priorities and relationship can quickly swing into chaos if your work takes on an inflated importance or work projects invade family or personal time.

In addition to the typical struggles that authors face in the publishing and blogging world, I also write books and freelance for Christians on a regular basis. When writing and Christianity converge, things can get a bit weird or, at the very least, complicated.

With your faith in the mix, typical writing tasks such as raising your profile as a freelancer or as an author bring up issues related to pride, fear, self-glorification, and love of money that are particularly relevant for Christians. As one author noted to me, Jesus said that the meek shall inherit the earth, but authors hoping to earn a living by attracting an audience need to promote themselves--a decidedly "non-meek" activity. In addition, the trends and practices in the Christian writing and publishing world may be surprising and different from the mainstream if you're not prepared for them.

Some may laugh maniacally and knowingly at the thought of people not expecting major issues in the Christian publishing world, while others, much like myself at first, may be completely shocked to find as many problems in the Christian publishing scene as anywhere else. That isn't to say that Christians are more dishonest or more conniving in their dealings. They most certainly aren't, and I've had many positive experiences over the years publishing and freelancing for Christians. Rather, the challenges and issues that come up in the Christian publishing and writing community are sometimes unique.

The expectations from fellow authors, readers, or businesses tend to be different when there's a mutual understanding that both parties are Christians. Every time I bring this up with fellow creative professionals, I'm met with knowing looks and stories that confirm there's something to this. If you're not ready for these unique challenges, you can be blindsided by the few who use faith as a cover for questionable business practices. Besides the financial impact of these abuses, writers of faith may be particularly demoralized if a pastor or previously well-regarded Christian leader exploits them. One friend had been hired to write for a church, working directly for a pastor. While the church finally paid his sizable invoice, it was 60 days late, each day past the original 30-day due date brought a crisis over whether pressure the pastor or the church for payment. He feared that would only make things worse. Believe me, if a writer or designer has the gall to second guess the integrity of a popular pastor or Christian leader, the public response will generally not be one of support for creative professional!

These stories of unique challenges that Christians face can range from reasonable conflicts of interest that are specific to businesses tied to religious values to questionable policies that veer dangerously close to being illegal. For instance, a Christian publisher may cancel your book project if you aren't on the same page over a hot-button theology topic. I ran into conflict with one editor when I suggested in a book project that pacifism was an important option for Christians to consider, especially in lieu of the "love your enemies" line from some guy. What started as a seemingly harmless conversation about a viable option for Christians ended with the publisher suggesting we cancel that book.

In retrospect, I'm glad we mutually agreed to end that project, but I certainly didn't see that conflict coming. On the wilder end of the spectrum, one author I know lost her book deal because she wrote a blog post that was critical of a biblical doctrine that bore no direct connection to her book. In addition, she never hid the fact that her denomination had no history of supporting that particular doctrine. The publisher didn't just cancel the deal. The publisher made several unreasonable demands that felt a bit more like attacking a heretic than terminating a contract in a professional manner.

The writing life has many challenges and unexpected obstacles along the way, but adding your faith to the mix brings about some unique situations. Whether you work primarily with other Christians or you take on general clients of all sorts, I want to offer a clear, at times bracing, picture of the writing life so that new writers aren't surprised by its challenges and experienced writers can normalize their experiences and find some support. I'm especially motivated to write about this because most writers are unaware of the worst case scenarios in publishing and freelancing, let alone how to rise above them. In my experience, it's hard to find stories of writers successfully overcoming adversity and the low points in a writing career.

The Highs and Lows of Writing Full and Part Time

I'm here to tell you that writing has many wonderful rewards and benefits, but it also has a myriad of traps, disappointments, and soul-crushing moments. It's actually just like any other career. You don't magically rise above the need to work hard and persevere through adversity by tapping away on a computer for a few hours each day. The grind of marketing and stress of meeting sales goals wears down many talented authors who publish commercially. The ups and down of querying editors can be stressful and a bit depressing, especially if you're relying on a book advance or article revenue to make ends meet. Depending on blog revenue and affiliate sales can be an exhausting cycle of content creation and social media promotion. More often than you would like, freelancing will lead you to ungrateful clients who will reward your hard work by replacing you with someone in-house or flaking out on invoices that are months overdue.

There are steps you can take to minimize these low points, and if you do hit them, you can most certainly rise above them and keep moving forward. I know that because I've hit all of these bumps in the road since I started writing seriously. I've been through a lot of low points and uncertainty, but at least as of this writing, I'm making a respectable part-time income through publishing and freelancing. I could make more if I didn't spend about half of my week at home with our kids, but that flexibility is obviously one of the advantages of writing for a living, even if it comes with plenty of other challenges and distractions.

If you do take the leap into writing for all or part of your income, I hope that my experiences can help you avoid some of the pitfalls, rise above the setbacks, and make decisions that will lead you to the most fulfilling aspects of the writing life. Whether you're hoping to entertain, minister, build extra income, or do a little of all three, writing can become a sustainable career that doesn't have to crush your soul or illuminate all of your fears and weaknesses. For those willing to remain vigilant about the challenges and pitfalls to their souls and careers, there are plenty of fulfilling options for writers.

You don't have to let your soul become a casualty of your writing work. You can find a sustainable pace and an authentic approach that protects your soul and provides a reasonable income. It may take a lot of time, planning, counsel, and work, but I believe you can get there. Let's get started with the most important issue facing any Christian who writes: finding your true self before you write another word.

CHAPTER 1

WRITING SUSTAINABLY

Finding Your Identity

Whether writing is a hobby, career, or part time project, it is unavoidably personal. Any work that draws on our personal creativity in such a direct way runs the risk of becoming a source for one's personal identity. If you have a book, article, or blog to promote, a bad review, insulting comment, or lack of interest from respected friends or colleagues can send your day into a tailspin. Even if you've enjoyed some success, the personal boost that comes from a high point will often be short-lived, and if you begin to raise your opinion of yourself based on your writing success, you'll soon find someone else who is enjoying more success.

There are few things in my life that mean more to me than my writing, and that is both my blessing and my curse. On the one hand, I can't stop myself from writing. I work hard to create space in my life to get writing done. It offers a way to process my thoughts, offers ways to serve others, and remains my most marketable skill. On the other hand, I've caught myself distracted and distant from my family when I've worried too much about a blog post, book release, or work project. The up and down nature of freelancing stole my joy for a season. I reasoned, "How can I enjoy time with my family when I need to land another client to make ends meet?" Money and success are cruel masters, and they'll demand steep sacrifices if constantly accumulating more becomes our focus.

Realistically speaking, we can make progress and changes in these areas, but to a certain degree, maintaining space for our spiritual lives, family, ministry, and writing requires ongoing maintenance. I've written in my book *Pray, Write, Grow* about the ways the daily Examen has offered a simple way to track where I'm at in this regard. For instance, over the course of several months I continuously listed my writing work as the best and most encouraging aspect of my day. Unfortunately, I wasn't looking at the moments I spent with my family as a source of joy or satisfaction because I was so worried about meeting sales goals, landing more work, and expanding my network. While the end goal, in part, was to help support our family financially, I lost sight of the beautiful moments reading books on our bed with our older boy or enjoying a rowdy family dinner where the youngest gets amped up. Believe me, when my mind is focused on meeting writing goals, it's obvious to everyone around me.

While I've found that part of the solution here requires addressing the unhealthy aspects of my mindset and the measures I use to define "success" or my personal identity, the most important step toward resolving my identity as a Christian who sustainably writes is rooted in my actions. Before I get to work in the morning, I try to pray the hours. After I read publishing articles in the evening, I pray with the Examen. When I'm done work, I shut down my computer and try to leave work behind. I don't answer client emails and avoid social media in the evenings and on the weekends as much as possible. I work on intentionally spending time with my family each day without giving my writing work a second thought. It's a fine line between being a dedicated, hard worker and a distracted over-worker some days. To a certain degree, I have to say "No" to myself. "No, I will not count my day a success if I land a high profile guest post at the expense of reading books to my son." "No, I will not let the stress of my new client invade my thoughts during dinner."

I can't speak definitively for every Christian writer, but I can say that the notion of a calling has helped me immensely as I sort out the balance between my work and my identity. My most important identity is based on God's opinion of me and my relationships with family and friends. My writing is something that I do because of a mix of calling and necessity to earn a living. I write out of what God is doing in and through me. However, I am not the same as my writing. I am defined by God's love for me, and the role I play as a husband, father, and friend. If I can't find fulfillment in those roles, writing won't help. In fact, writing will inevitably let me down because it simply isn't meant to offer that sort of fulfillment for the long term. It may fill that void for a season, but it will most certainly fade over time.

As I think and pray about my personal writing projects, especially in my blog posts, books, and newsletters, I routinely ask how I can write out of what God is speaking in my life. Topics such as being a work from home dad, healing from negative church experiences, and writing as a Christian have all weighed on my mind as I pray. Addressing these topics, then, isn't about creating a platform for myself per se--at least that's not the ultimate goal. I'm trying to write out of what God is doing in my life. I still work hard to make the writing good and to even promote it within my means, but the end result is to remain faithful to my calling, not dominating the publishing market or getting tons of clicks and likes.

This balance isn't always easy, I assure you. I have spent more time than I prefer to admit lamenting that certain books weren't praised by influential people or shared widely on social media. When one particular book project fizzled during its release week and was generally met by a shrug by people in my circles, a friend mentioned to me, "How many sales do you think you would have gotten from those endorsements and social media shares that you wanted?"

Honestly? Not that many. I was measuring my identity by my popularity and social media shares, not by my faithfulness. In fact, when I shared my insecurities about publishing with a few friends over a morning coffee meet up, I made the uncomfortable realization, right in their presence, that I'd placed so much value on the opinions of other authors or social media friends, I'd overlooked the encouragement of my friends in real life who see me every week. They'd supported me throughout my publishing work, but I hadn't valued their opinions and encouragement, even though they had prayed with me throughout the entire process and could affirm the ways God has led me. That was a huge mistake on my part.

I firmly believe that writers have quite a bit of power in controlling the impact of the crazy in their professional lives. We even bring the crazy on ourselves. The crazy is most often rooted in our personal identities and how we link our writing to our personal identity and worth.

By stepping back and grounding yourself in God's love and your closest relationships, you'll make one of the most important first steps in building a sustainable writing career. As Richard Rohr writes in *Immortal Diamond*, "Your True Self is who you are, and always have been in God . . . The great surprise and irony is that 'you,' or who you think you are, have nothing to do with its original creation or its demise. It's sort of disempowering and utterly empowering at the same time, isn't it? All you can do is nurture it." When you've finally stopped trying to please others or to make a name for yourself, you can rest more fully in your identity and write with more authenticity. It's a process that takes time, but you can certainly create an environment where that is more likely to happen than not.

For starters, beginning and ending every day on social media may offer a clue about your priorities. Try to spend some time in the morning and evening either reflecting on God's love for you, a short passage of scripture, or the events of the day that were encouraging or discouraging. Explore your insecurities and your accomplishments, and invite God into both of them.

Most importantly, every writer who wants to keep track of his or her soul needs some space to sit in awareness of God's presence. Nothing may happen or your life may change in a brief epiphany. The point is that we will find ourselves at the mercy of our writing work if we don't create a space for God to speak into our lives and to help us become grounded once again. If we dive into each day without an awareness of God's acceptance and calling for us, we may end up measuring our lives by the standards of others and even end up imitating others to the point that we lose sight of ourselves. That can be one of the most soul-crushing mistakes a writer can make.

Finding Your Voice and Style

I started writing seriously with a theology blog. I had just completed seminary, and it seemed like a natural place to channel my energy. I began to imitate the voice and style of my favorite theology blogs, expounding on deep theological concepts, especially the "intersection" of theology and culture. I had a little success, but as the years passed by, I struggled to keep the blog going. Theology as a writing topic gradually lost its appeal over the years, and I began to sell or give away many of my seminary textbooks. I routinely found myself veering into topics and even a style of writing that was quite different from the tone I'd set on the blog a few years before. I even began blogging about my anxieties over becoming a father, never touching on a single doctrine or theological controversy along the way. It was like two very different writers were competing for creative control. I also noticed that quite a few of my friends were starting new blogs, shutting down their old blogs, or pursuing different projects such as podcasts and newsletters. I began to wonder if my struggle to write on my theology blog could be solved by a similar shift.

Looking back, I can see that I had made the common mistake of imitating the voice and style of other writers instead of finding my own. You can imitate another writer for a little while, but it will soon wear you down and kill your creativity. The work of writing will feel like a chore rather than a joy. While each writer switches up projects or blogs for a variety of reasons, I needed to begin reshaping my identity around my personal writing interests rather than the confines of theology. It's not that I didn't have some thoughts about theology and my beliefs. Rather, I wanted to explore those topics on my own terms and in my own ways. I realized that I wasn't a theologian first and foremost. And let's be honest here, a blog post by a seasoned Bible scholar explaining a controversial topic in five succinct points will carry a lot more weight than anything a guy like me with an Master of Divinity can muster, ever if I may have constructive ideas to contribute. Imitating a Bible scholar wasn't just adding to my personal misery. It was holding back my career as a writer.

When I switched to a blog centered on my own interests and under my own name, I immediately sensed the creative freedom to explore particular topics that had previously felt out of bounds at my old blog. In addition, it finally made sense to advertise my book editing and website content services on my site. I was a writer first and foremost, not a theologian.

These days I talk to a lot of writers who feel like they need to follow the precise blueprints for success that others have laid out. My advice is to only focus on the things you like to do and stop worrying about completely imitating someone else. I know one writer who was miserable as a Christian blogger, so he dropped his blog, took his faith offline, and pursued copywriting projects that were more in line with his personal interests. Other writers have dramatically changed their websites, launched podcasts, or opted to send out weekly emails or "Tiny Letters" to their subscribers. As I began to plan out my long term writing career for at least the next 5-10 years, I began to ruthlessly cut out anything that contributed to my misery. Mind you, as I invested more time into writing and gathering subscribers for my newsletter, I subscribed to several leading newsletters in my field in order to learn from my favorites.

It's way more fun and sustainable over the long term to just be myself. That isn't to say I don't try to think of writing projects that appeal to readers. I also axe projects that aren't coming together. However, I'm not going to pursue an idea that could be successful if it makes me hate sitting down to write every day. If an idea keeps coming up when I write notes and brainstorm, then I know I've hit on something worth pursuing.

Independent publishing legend Hugh Howey wrote in his post "KDP Is for Chumps" that publishing through Kindle Direct Publishing on his own has allowed him to make money writing books that he would be doing for free anyway. That is a refreshing way to look at one aspect of writing! Would you post on a blog or write a book for free any way?

There's still a place for getting paid for a website, book, or freelancing work, with most writers picking up the latter to make ends meet. However, if you start a creative project that becomes a source of misery and guilt, perhaps its time to switch things up a bit. Don't worry about losing the SEO, fans, and followers you've accumulated over the years. If you tap into something that you really care about, people will eventually find you again, and, as a bonus, you won't resent them when they ask for more content. In fact, drumming up new creative ideas is the most demanding part of writing work, so you better love what you're writing about if you want to last long term.

Finding Ideas

I've never been very interested in blog posts or books that offer prompts for heaps and mountains of writing ideas. If I want to think of writing ideas, the only way forward, in my experience, is to write and jot down ideas during little bits of free time. I'm sympathetic to folks who feel like they need a jumpstart, but a writer's insecurity about where to begin may have more to do with how that writer spends time each day than with that writer's ability to think of topics.

Every writer fears that the next book won't come together or that readers will hate it--even bestselling authors speak of their anxiety attacks over writing the next book. Perhaps you're struggling with doubts and fears of your abilities. There could be something to these doubts and fears! You may need to work on your writing and read books that help with your craft. I've spent plenty of time reading and rereading a favorite book just to get a sense of how the author structured a story or presented an idea. There's no doubt that you may have room to improve. We all do.

When we think of how to come up with ideas, consider whether you're developing a process that nurtures writing ideas rather than fearing you'll never come up with them. Without the right process in place, you certainly won't come up with writing ideas. Here's one way to start.

What do you do when you wait for something?

Is your first instinct to flip on the radio, to check out social media, or to start texting people? Do you ever have a block of time during the day to jot down ideas? Do you have a place where you could easily write down ideas and follow up on them later? Do you ever let your mind shift into neutral and let it wander?

Anyone can sit down and scribble down some ideas or take some time for a free-write to explore an idea. The ideas on your list may be good or they may be terrible. If you keep at it enough, certain ideas will stick with you. If you stop filling your free time with television, radio, social media, and video games, you'll even have a chance to ponder them further and keep developing them. Writing isn't just something you do when you sit down with a pen or computer. It needs to become a lifestyle where you let your mind wander while taking a walk or standing in line or doing the dishes. While there's nothing wrong with checking your smart phone while in line or watching some television, our problem is that these things become our constant defaults. It's really easy to avoid any type of self-reflection.

Trust the writing process, and don't panic if it takes some time.

I write in *Pray, Write, Grow* that cultivating prayer practices can also help us uncover the very things we need to write about. In my experience, prayer and writing create a self-sustaining circle where prayer uncovers what I need to write about and writing provides clarity on what I should pray about. Both practices provide a way to sort out my thoughts, and by the time I'm done praying or reflecting for my writing work, I often have a handle on which ideas need to be developed. I often end up with plenty of half-written blog posts, abandoned articles, discarded book descriptions. That strikes me as a good sign. If I think everything I write is pure gold, then I'm going to really disappoint my readers!

In fact, sometimes I review my lists of ideas or unfinished drafts and notice that I've written something that may need to be written, but it doesn't have to be written by me. A good idea isn't necessarily an "Ed-idea." Writers can easily fall into the trap of trying to fulfill someone else's calling or role because we see the need for something and then try to fill it, even if we aren't passionate about it, experienced, or knowledgeable enough to write in a way that is helpful. In fact, we may get into the project and realize that we resent it.

For many of us, we started writing when everything we produced was free, and that can actually be a saving grace when it comes to launching a book or a website. You really have to believe in something if you're going to invest hour after hour into it without any promise of pay. For instance, don't begin a book project unless you're convinced that the book needs to exist, even if you can't make money from it. Most first books earn little to no money for their authors any way, so you'll often find that writing the book you need to write will guard you from any potential disappointments. Whatever the outcome, if you've been faithful to your calling, then you can celebrate any outcome.

After you hit publish for a blog post, article, or book, don't panic if the next idea is slow to take shape. There's more going on in your mind than you realize. The more you explore an idea, the deeper it can take you. The more you invest in your writing, the more you'll need to carve out time to be alone with your thoughts or to process them further. It's true that writers often find themselves unable to stay away from writing, but writing ideas can also be encouraged to take shape if we give them room. The "work" of writing isn't just to sit down and write. That's a major part of it, but there's also the demanding task of becoming the sort of people who are able to write.

Even if we set aside enough time to write, we can also develop more writing ideas if we commit to regularly reading authors who stretch, inform, and inspire us. I read quite a few books and articles about prayer and publishing, and they regularly push me to change my prayer and work habits. Those practices introduce new ideas and push me to examine parts of myself I may have overlooked. As I interact with these outside perspectives, my writing shifts and evolves.

If I could say one thing about the process of finding writing ideas, it's that writers hold the majority of the power in themselves. No one has to rely on prompts, articles, or books to find the next idea. They can certainly help, but they aren't a good long term plan. By planning your schedule carefully, regularly taking time to jot down ideas, and intentionally reading books and articles that will inspire you to write and provide new ideas, you'll set yourself up for a healthier approach to reliably develop new writing ideas each day.

Besides, the goal for writers is to write sustainably for

the long term. We don't want to burn out or grow increasingly miserable as we invest in our work and in ourselves as writers. In fact, if we don't invest in ourselves and give ourselves time for rest and recovery, we'll soon hit a season of struggle.

Finding Restoration

Whether you primarily write books or freelance for your income, there is a constant temptation to continually look ahead to the next project. To a certain degree, this is responsible and even understandable. I genuinely love writing. When I'm almost done a book, I get a predictable itch during the final copy edits to begin the next one. By the time I'm uploading the final version to online retail sites, I usually have an outline and a few thousands words done on my next book. Even while wrapping up this project's first draft, I completed outlines and sample chapters for two other book projects. It's hard to stop myself from thinking ahead!

While it's commendable to plan ahead when you're relying on writing to provide an income, writing can also take on too prominent a role in our lives. We need space for prayer, family, and other life-giving pursuits. Keeping clear boundaries around each area is a large part of the battle. I need long stretches of focused time to really dig into a writing project--with a minimum of two to three hours at a time being ideal in the best of times. However, I also need time away. Over the years I have found it most difficult to give myself a season of restoration. I spend so much time looking ahead that I've failed to care for myself both spiritually and professionally.

God gives us the Sabbath because rest is good for us, not because God likes to make up rules. Jesus said that the

Sabbath is for the benefit of humanity. In fact, limitations are really good for us. Think about this for a moment: when God gave the nation of Israel laws for their society, God mandated a day of rest for everyone. This wasn't a suggestion or a best-practices manual. This was a vitally important law that stood at the heart of the society's health. God also mandated a year of rest every seven years, which is pretty staggering to think about in a rural/agrarian society. Taking a season of rest was a major leap of faith.

At the heart of the Sabbath command is a message that every worker needs to hear: We are more than our work. In our society today it's common to ask each other, "What do you do?" as a means of introduction, as if the answer to that question automatically tells us the most important thing about another person. Perhaps a more revealing question would be "Who or what do you love?" Even "What do you like to do?" or "How do you spend your time?" could give us a better sense of another person's true identity. We need rest from our work because our work isn't who we are and our work isn't God. Work can most certainly become an important part of our identities, and God can be present throughout the workday, but God calls us to step back completely at least one day a week because we are more than our productivity.

I have felt the tension of work becoming a god of sorts. I have struggled with relying on my work for my sense of meaning and for our family's provision to the point that I haven't trusted God. A Sabbath day cuts me out of that delusion. When I finally have to stop working, I have an opportunity to see the ways my life has swung out of balance.

For all of my misgivings about the ways some churches operate like consumer-based businesses or country clubs, there is much to be said about the way that a good church service can turn our focus away from ourselves and our own pursuits. By participating in prayer and the study of scripture in a community, we can reorient ourselves with God and see the needs of others around us. If we really want to move into a healthy place, we'll even take the initiative and begin serving others. I write in my book *Hazardous* that we grow spiritually when we step out in faith and take risks that force us to rely on God. In addition, moving out of our own circles of concern and sharing in the difficulties of others may be the best thing for us. Jesus said those who mourn are blessed and we read in Ecclesiastes 7:2 "It is better to go to a house of mourning than to go to a house of feasting, for death is the destiny of everyone; the living should take this to heart."

That's some pretty heavy stuff to think about, but it is far more tragic to go through life fretting about rejection letters, low readership, or snubs from influential authors as if these were the most important things. Sharing in the struggles and suffering of others may not sound all that restoring or refreshing, but this solidarity with others isn't just vitally important, it also saves us from ourselves. Mind you, we don't want to serve someone just to give ourselves a reality check! This is merely a side benefit. We serve others both because they need our help and this is precisely the type of life that Jesus modeled for us. I heard a speaker in college share "Stop asking 'What Would Jesus Do?' and start asking 'What *did* Jesus do?'" There's no mistaking that Jesus spent a good deal of time helping people who were either disreputable sinners or struggling because of illness. If we can't stop our work to serve others, we run the risk of tricking ourselves into thinking our work is the most important thing there is. When difficult days inevitably come, the result could be devastating. Regular Sabbath and service are our best guards against this crash.

In order to maintain a regular Sabbath and periods of rest, I have found that I need a routine or rhythm to my writing life. Habits in particular help. I need to know that every Sunday I'll wake up and NOT work. The day is dedicated to family and church. When I've volunteered, it has helped to choose something that is scheduled, such as prison ministry one night a week or one day a month, or helping at the food pantry one day a month. I also need to know that my computer is shut down at the end of the work day, and I'm going to avoid interacting on social media in the evening when I should be reading, gardening, or spending time with my family.

If you have a clear sense of who you are and what truly matters, you'll have a much healthier starting point for your writing work. You'll also be in a stronger position to courageously take the risks of writing.

Finding Courage

The first fear that every writer must face is rejection.

When I started out as a new writer, I took the rejection emails pretty hard. I was sick to my stomach for an entire day, feeling like a complete failure. However, in many ways, these editors were just telling me the truth that I feared. My book ideas were rarely good enough, and I certainly didn't have the experience they were looking for in an author. That didn't mean they were telling me to stop writing, to stop developing ideas, or to even cease pitching books or articles to them. I filled in that part of the message myself. They had only rejected my current project. The truth is that my rejection was but one of many, many more "No's" that would follow.

Sometimes "No" is the best word for us, even if we genuinely fear it. For people of faith who genuinely believe that our creative talents are gifts from God and that we should offer our best work to God as we put them into practice. I have yet to meet a writer who started out with a clear idea of what it takes to publish a book or article successfully, let alone to successfully publish high quality blog posts. Is there any field where a beginner can start out with a high level of expertise? If you're getting rejected at the start, that's just par for the course. Mind you, rejection is always par for the course for writers--it never, ever stops. However, it will be particularly common at the start.

All of that to say, adversity can be good for us. Sometimes hearing "no" is the only way we'll push ourselves to publish something better. That isn't true for everyone, as some may take a rejection to heart and consider giving up, but I have found that I can turn rejection around into either a prompting to work harder or to at least try something else.

Besides, If you're trying to write out of a sense of calling or ministry, then you may well be in for a lot of adversity and discouragement. A "calling" or "mission" from God is often an invitation to suffer, struggle, and face impossible odds. Not that we're aiming to become as epic as a Hebrew prophet, but how many prophets in the Bible were greeted by their contemporaries as heroes or important spokespersons? In the majority of cases their writings were saved by a small group of followers, and they only became "mainstream" years later as their wisdom stood the test of time. You simply can't predict what readers will say or how they will respond, but if you struggle to find a willing audience at first, you're in good company.

In general, writing can be terrifying. New freelancers fear feedback from their clients. New bloggers fear the first critical comments or social media replies. New authors fear the first critical review. Putting our personal thoughts and experiences out there leaves us vulnerable and exposed. The critical comments and reviews can stick with us, especially if we've based our identity on the opinions of others or pleasing others.

I have personally managed many of the fears and discouragements that come from writing through two key mindsets: desperation and calling. Ironically, I really fought against the concept of writing full time for a really, really long time. I tried out everything else that I thought I possibly could do, and while I was responsible and competent, nothing came close to writing. While writing I have always sensed that it's my true north. I also felt like an imposter doing everything else.

When I started going to writing conferences and chatting with my peers, I felt like I had finally found my tribe. Every career has bad days and downsides, so if I have to manage a bit of social media crazy, a critical comment from a client, and the occasional negative book review, that's a price I have to be willing to pay. I'll take my worst day as a writer over my best days in the other careers I tried out. When I was finally desperate enough to try writing full time, I finally saw that my discontent in every other career was rooted in the fact that I instinctively knew I should be doing something very different with my life. That sort of desperation to try something else can give you a strikingly high threshold for rejection and pain.

Once I let myself start writing regularly with an eye to making a career of it, I found that I also had a stronger sense of calling. It became easier to write and to take risks because I had a strong sense of God calling me to keep working at it and to keep launching new projects. Deep in the back of my mind I sensed that I would always write, whether or not I had a contract with a publisher. While I have certainly craved the support and expertise of publishers at certain points in my career, there is something reassuring about this commitment. I would always write. No one could stop that.

Pain and fear can be managed, and the more you face them, the stronger you'll become. It may take longer than you like to build up your strength, and, at least in my case, you only notice that growth by looking back over the long term. In addition, once you've endured the pain of rejection, a bad review, or online conflict several times, you start to learn that it will pass and develop ways to cope. It may leave you changed in small or large ways, but once you face rejection or a bad review, you'll become stronger for the next one--and there certainly will be a next one.

Along the way you'll find that sometimes you need a bit of space between your professional profile and your personal life. Then again, some of the best friends you'll make along the way are the ones who can support you in your darkest hours. Finding that balance between your public and private life will go a long way in making your writing career sustainable.

Dividing Your Public and Private Lives

There are so many ways that writing and its accompanying social media outreach can creep into our personal lives. It has been a matter of trial and error for me over the years. I know what kind of person I want to be: I want to be present for my friends and family, prayerful and centered in the moment. I don't want to be scrolling through my smartphone while with my kids are at the playground or during family dinner. However, a project that hits a snag, a massive book release, or a financial need that prompts me to drum up new business can routinely provide exceptions to my boundaries. Before I realize it, I'm immersed in an email and mentally cut off from the people in the same room. I'm forever making adjustments, setting new boundaries, and even taking temporary fasts in order to reset my habits.

Such ongoing adjustments are especially necessary now

because the skill sets that writers need can be so vast and the number of tasks we need to take on seem endless. You can wear yourself out doing many things poorly and then have little left to give your family and closest friends, leaving you frustrated and despairing about ever making progress.

This doesn't have to be an either/or type of situation. I believe that healthy relationships can be important in both real life and in online life. The challenge is that our most important relationships and our personal health can suffer because of the unique challenges of a career in writing. For instance, releasing a book can occupy a significant amount of emotional energy and mental space. When I've been releasing a new commercial book, I've also been notably less present to my family simply because I kept thinking about what was working and what wasn't working and whether I should try something else. When I haven't had enough freelance work, I've made the mistake of either worrying about it during family time or pushing myself to drum up new opportunities through my networks, losing my time for personal restoration or time with my family.

In the vast majority of cases, I have found that "online" friends are always far more kind, fun, and enjoyable in person. Some of my online friends have provided us with a place to stay while traveling or met up with us for dinner, while others have stayed at our home while they were on the road. These connections can be amazing and life-giving, but the lure of checking in with a friend or 20 on social media can also pull us away from our family and the friends we interact with daily.

Writers today are surrounded by articles listing 50 things you can do to promote your book or the 10 essential social media tools or some other list of things they aren't doing or need to do in order to be successful with their work. I have stopped reading such articles, unless I'm just scanning them for a new idea or tool that could replace something I'm already doing. I try to balance what I can do (with both my abilities and time), what I like to do, and what may actually work to get my writing done and to share it with others. The best guides to managing my work/life balance are the ones who help discern what works and what doesn't work for me.

For instance, I set schedules and develop habits, rely on automated social media tools, and put boundaries around my working and publicity time to help me work sustainably and productively. I will not get everything done each week. I never will. However, I can at least focus on getting the most important work done and guard my most important relationships. That is the big shift for me: social media marketing and networking are not the end all and be all for writers. Being healthy people who do good work must come first. How you connect with readers must follow all of that. I don't neglect social media, but I also don't measure my progress as if it's the most important thing I do.

Social media can become addicting both during family time and writing time. There are clear benefits to social media for writers. We find connections with our peers, market our work, find new clients, and keep in touch with distant friends and family. We can also visit social media far too often when we hit a rough patch of writing or when we're spending time with family or friends. It's just a quick flip of a smartphone or adding a new browser tab, but it's pulling our attention away from our family, our work, and time that could be given to spiritual or personal restoration. In fact, many studies are beginning to suggest that constant social media use results in anxiety and a poor outlook on life. The pressure to keep up with the latest news from everyone, to reply to every message, and to maintain a presence as an author or a creative professional can wear us down if we don't impose limits and breaks on ourselves. Let's face it, we all present our best sides on social media, so it's also easy to begin envying the perfect life someone else has while we struggle to make ends meet, to keep our family relationships in tact, or to keep ourselves in a healthy place spiritually.

Many writers I know have taken to strict limits around their social media usage and even employ blocks on social media in order to remove the temptation. Some have given up social media completely for a season, such as Lent. That may sound like more of a liability than a positive step, but the truth is that you won't preserve your soul, write excellent material, or remain in healthy relationships by prioritizing social media or sharing as much as you possibly can. You may not grow a social media following as fast as some people, but if your goal is to maintain a healthy soul while doing excellent work, you need clear boundaries around everything that could drain time away from those two areas and undermine your ability to respond to others in a healthy way. I even know one writer who regularly suspends his social media accounts if he senses himself entering into an unhealthy place.

I try to be extremely discerning about my social media connections, and if anyone strikes me as too toxic or combative, I immediately disengage. If I want to misunderstand someone and dehumanize them quickly, there's no better way to do that than to engage is a social media fight.

From where I sit, the most important thing you can do as a writer, especially if you want to have a blog or social media platform, is to divide your professional personality from your family life. That isn't to say you can't share some pictures of your kids or talk about personal issues. Rather, you need to work with your family on setting clear boundaries so that you avoid the temptation of living too much in your professional writing sphere or violating the privacy of family members. I confess that I'm probably more on the private end of the spectrum. My Instagram pictures are protected because they're mostly of my kids. I delete the majority of the Instagram friend requests that come my way. I'm very careful about who can see what I post on Facebook. I keep Twitter VERY general. Writing is hard enough without social media drama and the ways that it can disrupt your personal life. By all means use it to connect with readers and colleagues. In fact, I actually implore you to connect with colleagues on social media, but don't think you can find a healthy balance without a bit of thought and planning.

A bad contract, a failed book project, a social media misstep, or any other number of setbacks could send your professional life spiraling downward for a season. The less you tie your private life with your professional life, the better off you'll be in times of adversity. You need friends and family who are connected with you personally and can support you when your writing career hits a rough patch. Most importantly, relationships outside of your writing career will keep you grounded in what's most important. While I thought that serving in prison ministry for a number of years was all about helping the men behind bars heal and start over, I also received the tremendous blessing of seeing how much the issues I gave myself to each day online were often peripheral. The controversy du jour evaporated once I sat next to a former drug offender who was about to be released and was praying fervently for God to keep him clean in the coming months.

We need something other than our social media profiles, blog posts, and books. While these can be vitally important projects and ministries that help a large number of people, our relationships with God, with family, and

people in need become vital in creating a truly resilient identity. The greatest strengths of writers may well reside in what we do while away from our work.

CHAPTER 2

DEALING WITH ADVERSITY

Fears that Writers Face

There are two major mistakes you can make as a writer: assuming everyone will love your writing or assuming everyone will hate your writing. The truth is somewhere in between those extremes, as no writer can make every single reader happy. We've all had that experience when we pick up a widely recommended book and toss it aside after a few chapters. Most of us have also had the experience of recommending a book to a family member or friend and later hearing that they thought it was terrible.

If you're just starting out as a writer, you may have more readers or colleagues offering critical opinions of your work. Thats usually a good sign. If you're new to writing and everyone loves your work, you may need to find people who can help you improve. You'll especially need lots of feedback and revising before publishing a major work. Even then you will almost certainly receive negative reviews. Worse than that, if you're just getting started, you may run the risk of no one reading your work. While it's natural to fear what editors or readers may say, criticism can often help you improve if received from the right perspective.

The most important point I stress to new writers is that you're beginning a process when you work on a book or any major writing project. A book is not a linear process where you make an outline, hammer out 50,000 words, and then start selling copies. Books call for revisions, cutting, and moving throughout multiple drafts. Writing an article takes constant revising, sharpening, and deleting. A blog post may take shape over the course of a few days and a website may unfold over the course of several weeks. It could look quite different from the original draft by the time it goes live.

Commit yourself to the process of writing, not getting it right the first time or fearing that you'll never get it perfect. You need to make each draft as good as it can be, trusting that through either personal or outside critique, you can make it better. If you can't get a book or article right after two or three tries, there's no rule saying you can't try again or that an editor couldn't help you rework the piece. The main difference between average writers and great writers isn't in their first drafts. While certain writers may come up with better ideas or outlines at the outset, it's in the trenches of revisions that great work can take shape. I've often noticed that toward the end of a second draft I often capture the precise voice I want to use in a book, and then the quality of the book hinges on how well I can integrate that voice into each chapter's rewrites.

Oftentimes I'll discover that my writing has drifted from

my core audience, and I need to make revisions just for them. I usually try to write with either a one-sentence summary of my book handy or the article guidelines from a magazine editor when I'm working on projects. I need to be constantly reoriented by the big picture while working on the details. This is especially true with a book. You may be making a fantastic point that is absolutely true, but it may be completely irrelevant to your readers or you may be adopting a tone that is completely inaccessible for your readers. Whether outlining, writing a first draft, or revising, I try to return to these basic questions: Who am I writing for? What am I saying to them? And What do I want them to do after reading my work?

As you imagine these readers, you may fear their responses to your writing. You may fear that it's all falling flat. However, you need to begin by filling up page after page. After you give yourself some raw materials, you can return to them a few days, weeks, or even months later to see them with new eyes. Even returning to a project after a night's sleep will help you spot problems and work toward solutions that would have been unimaginable a day earlier. Sometimes the best solution is to start from scratch with a brand new outline, while other times you need to start cutting and pasting sections.

It's a process that will veer from one direction to another at times. You may end up deleting more than you keep. Ernest Hemingway once quipped that it took him 90 pages of terrible writing before composing a single page of masterpiece.

As you begin the writing process, remember this: nothing is wasted. If you want to write sustainably for years to come, every word you write is an investment in yourself as a writer. Stop focusing on your output each month as the measure of your success. It's more important that you're learning and developing: creating healthy habits for outlining, writing first drafts with reckless abandon, and then revising with patience and awareness of your audience.

What's the worst thing that could happen?

Well? Lots of things...

Critical Feedback

If you try to attract new readers through a blog or through social media, you'll expose yourself to the give and take of readers. So many of these tools can benefit authors who want to reach their readers directly, but there is a dark side in some cases. I know several writers who have actually quit blogging or scaled back their social media presence because of the vitriol of comments and the insulting comments and messages they receive. These range from sexist and threatening comments directed at women to theological policing and bullying. I know writers who have been approached by church leaders over their blog posts and social media updates, gotten into spats with one-time friends in the comment section, and were even attacked with hashtag campaigns. It's so incredibly easy to cross the line from disagreeing to dehumanizing when you're only dealing with an avatar and the opinions of that avatar. A flesh and blood person is reduced to a picture with ideas that must be attacked and dismantled.

On the less sensational end of things, blog readers may still chime in to voice their indifference, to question your faith, or to criticize your life choices. Social media will expose you to family members, friends, and even strangers who may take offense at your views. Before you receive your first critical comment from a publisher, magazine editor, or reviewer, blogging and posting on social media about certain topics could expose you to a great deal of critical or negative feedback.

The first step toward managing the crazy of online interactions is to avoid dumping gasoline on potentially incendiary conversations when possible. Once I stopped bringing up politics on social media and blocked a few repeat offenders, my anxiety about social media dropped significantly. It's not that I don't hold strong opinions on certain hot button issues. I certainly do. Rather, I believe that someone like myself won't change the world by railing for or against any big picture issue on social media. I'm all for passing along information that could help fuel needed social change. However, I'm more interested in taking specific action for a particular issue, whether that's praying, making a donation, voting for a specific law, or volunteering my time. In fact, I've heard from several activists and organizers who lament that social media "slacktivism" has become a major problem. While they certainly want help spreading the word about their work and they want people to be passionate about their causes, they don't want activism to stop in a Facebook comment thread or with a retweet on Twitter.

Besides resolving to avoid unnecessary controversy, we can also preserve our mental and spiritual healthy by resolving to respond to each and every comment with kindness while avoiding all personal attacks. We all need to set our own limits here, but I have often found that it's extremely helpful to wait at least 12 hours before responding to a critical, combative, or ignorant comment or reply. Going back to my old school blogging roots, one of the first and most popular Christian bloggers suggested that we treat our sites as a front porch or living room conversation. If someone stepped out of line in that setting, we'd think nothing of asking that person to speak respectfully or leave. While the comparison isn't perfect, the spirit of that rule challenges us to humanize every person who interacts with us online. That means my role is to be a good host who addresses troublemakers and remains respectful to all parties. I have the responsibility to set my own comment guidelines and to enforce them. An insulting or combative commenter is creating a toxic atmosphere for everyone else. I've found that reaching out to an aggressive commenter often results in a positive conversation, and if others see that I'm working to create a space to have a safe conversation, they'll be more likely to share their thoughts.

In fact, oftentimes people come across completely differently online compared to their manner in real life. I've found that the surest way to misunderstand someone and what they believe is to engage in an argument on social media or in blog comments. I've also seen these online arguments spiral out of control as one misunderstanding or assumption piles on top of the other and soon people are just shooting barbs at each other without sight of the original discussion. This is especially bad on Twitter where it's hard to discuss a complex topic in a series of 140-character tweets, especially when you can isolate a screen shot of a single tweet and share it widely.

Most importantly, engaging in online arguments can be really bad for your soul. You can begin to obsess over what people think of you. Insults can sting. You don't have to search hard to find stories about the devastating impact of online shaming and attacks. The less you invest in online fights, the healthier you'll be for the long term and the more you can invest in the actual work of writing.

Rejection by Agents and Editors

I find it hard to imagine that anyone could write a worst first book proposal than my own. Filled with optimism and high hopes about my dream of publishing a book, I followed the publisher's guidelines and shot off an email with the blessing of a graduate school professor who served as a benefactor of sorts. Perhaps because of his connection with my project, they actually responded to my query. I almost wish they hadn't.

"What credentials do you have to write this book?"

I spent a few days licking my wounds after reading that one.

While I tried to remember that "No" was a very likely answer my query, I didn't imagine that an editor would even question whether I even had any business publishing a book in the first place. It was an honest and fair response to a naive rookie writer. My dreams of publishing a book seemed doomed right from the start.

I could have taken several different directions at that point in my career, but since I knew nothing about publishing and appeared to be way in over my head, I took up another professor on his offer to make contact with his agent. The agent wrote back right away. He saw potential in my raw proposal, limited experience, and non-existent marketing ideas.

Most authors hoping to publish commercially opt to work through agents in order to take advantage of their contacts and expertise. The majority of commercial publishers prefer to work through an agent in order to ensure the proposals and manuscripts they receive are better targeted to their needs and of a higher quality. While working with an agent makes it slightly more likely that a publisher will take a chance on your book, since agents aren't interested in spending their time querying books that don't have a prayer, it does add a layer of work on the path to publication. Before you can even look into querying an editor, you need to get an agent on your side.

A struggling author once asked me when he should give up on querying agents in the hope of publishing commercially. He had read stories of bestselling authors who each overcame an incredible number of rejections before finding fame and fortune in publishing. That question is nearly impossible to answer, but it may help to begin with a question about your goals.

How will an agent help you accomplish your publishing goals?

I know one author who signed with an agent because he didn't want to worry about the negotiations and contract terms with a publisher. I signed with an agent in order to improve the presentation of my proposals. Other authors look to agents primarily for coaching and long term career advice. If you plan to work with commercial publishers, an agent can minimize conflict during negotiations, help you get better terms on your deal, and smooth out any disagreements that come up while working on your project.

Agents are often bombarded with queries, so you may not receive a response right away or ever if you have queried a popular agent. Rejection may feel like silence, which is a pretty terrible feeling no matter how justified a swamped an agent may be in not replying. However, even if you do land an agent, that doesn't mean everything will be smooth sailing.

Agents can offer valuable advice, make important connections, and guide you in making your work more professional, but not every author and agent are a great fit. Some agents may have a few all star clients who absorb more of their attention than a new author or an author with a smaller following. Other agents may simply have different expectations than the authors who hire them. Conflict could arise about how often an agent should get in touch, how aggressive an agent should be in pitching editors, whether an agent should try to auction off a book, or how much time an agent should spend advising an author on his/her career.

If you're searching for an agent right now, consider what you expect from your agent, what other authors receive from their agents, and what could work best for you at this point in your career. An agent could be among the best sources of perspective throughout your writing career, so make sure you choose an agent who feels like a good fit for your personality and career goals. If you feel like you're falling behind or at least going no where, an agent can offer the insight you need to get yourself back on track. If you don't feel like you can ask an agent for the help you need, then you may want to consider working with someone else.

Even when the best case scenario happens and you've managed to sign on with an agent due to a connection in your network or through a compelling query letter, an editor or marketing team at a publisher could reject your proposal. I've made so many promising connections with editors only to see a proposal get shot down by a publisher's editorial board or marketing team meeting. I've heard things such as: Not the right project. Not enough platform. Already have something. Not a good fit. Not a good project. This book already exists. We tried something like this book once, and it failed.

These replies are on the gentler end of things. There's also a chance that an editor could respond with a pretty strongly worded rejection.

Whether a rejection email is strong or gentle, it can be devastating to see your hopes and dreams getting shot down. If you've been through this with several editors, you may face the possibility that you need to shelve this project. It can be demoralizing to think you've finally accomplished something only to find that you need to start over again from scratch and develop a better idea.

There is no professional career where someone can just jump in and immediately find success. When I see new authors struggling to write a proposal, I can really relate with them. A proposal balances marketing copy and excellent book writing--two extremely different skills in one document! This isn't something you can dominate right from the start. Expect a learning curve, expect to shelve several projects along the way.

Almost every successful author has several projects that didn't make the cut initially. Honestly? All of them would tell you that, in retrospect, they're grateful their earliest works didn't get published. They would have been eviscerated by reviewers and would have struggled to meet their sales goals.

Keep a running file of book ideas, and chip away at outlines and opening chapters when you can. The more in-progress material you have, the better. I know what it feels like to hit a wall with agent or editor queries. In fact, as I looked over my sales data from my commercial projects, I realized that I wasn't getting enough traction with readers in the traditional way. Editors were interested in my proposals, but nothing I sent was "the right fit." While I still work with an agent, I published several independent projects to see how things would go. Having resolved that I would write no matter what, I found that removing myself from the proposal writing and querying process eliminated a time-consuming and distasteful aspect of my writing work.

Mind you, independent publishing isn't for slackers. I still have someone edit my work, I still seek out readers for early feedback, and all of the marketing is on me. The advantage that I've found comes from being able to manage every aspect of the process on my own, picking my editors, jumping on promotions when the opportunities arise, and moving each project at my own pace. I have far fewer relationships to manage as well, which could get exhausting when publishers refused to explore new marketing ideas or work with an endorser's limited timetable.

Whether you choose to be selective about your agent, decide to work with whichever agent shows interest, or strike out on your own as an independent or hybrid author, your writing career could hit other roadblocks and challenges. This is especially true if you sign with an agent who looks at your marketing platform and suggests that you write for magazines or online publications.

Rejected by Magazine Editors

When I started out in magazine writing, I imagined that I was both growing my platform and developing a source of side income that would supplement my book publishing work. I didn't necessarily have a burning desire to get published in a magazine. It was always a means to an end for me, and that was a big problem right from the start.

Magazine writing can be particularly demanding and time-consuming, especially if you don't have the experience or desire to learn the best practices. While I certainly have made some money writing for magazines and know people who have done quite well for themselves writing for magazines, I don't personally pursue magazine writing as a significant source of income at this time unless an editor reaches out to me.

One magazine editor explained to me that articles in a magazine need to be written in a fairly similar voice and style, which can be challenging when you're bringing in a group of freelance writers. This challenge alone suggests a major problem that new writers face when pitching magazines: if you don't read the magazine regularly, it will show in your pitch.

So let's imagine that you have ten magazines you want to pitch, that's ten magazines you should read in your spare time in order to get a sense of what they publish and how to write your piece. Then you need to work on pitches to each magazine that are carefully crafted to fit the voice of the magazine. Even if these magazines do offer a payment, it's typically on publication, which could be at least six months away from when you pitch, and the chances of your pitch getting selected out of the many they receive are pretty slim. And even if you do get selected, you could end up doing tons of revisions to your article as needs or available space change. If you're getting paid by the word, each round of edits could shave away from your final check. Sometimes editors end up cutting pieces when new issues come up that are more urgent. Other times the whole magazine may go out of business.

When I started freelancing full time, I had a book contract and two magazine columns. Within three months of quitting my day job, I had lost all three due to the volatility of the publishing market. With just a few emails the income sources I'd built up over the past three years completely disappeared when I needed them the most.

The people I know who have thrived the most in the magazine market have training in journalism, know how to pitch stories quickly, and have invested significant time in writing articles for publication. When I have had success at pitching magazine editors, it's typically because I reached out to them personally over email or over Twitter to ask if they have any specific needs based on what I've written. Opening a bit of dialogue on social media with editors and then emailing them two or three ideas that I could write up provided a low-risk way for me to pitch ideas without overwhelming them with emails. Editors have almost always replied to my tweets or direct messages on Twitter, and once they've offered a bit of feedback on what they need, they're also far more likely to respond to my submissions. This has ended up saving both of us a ton of time, although it certainly isn't a guarantee that my article pitches will be accepted!

While I'm not saying bloggers or authors shouldn't pursue magazine publication, it's worth considering how far outside of their skill set magazine article writing may be. It is completely different to work on a book or a blog post where you have far more creative control about how to present your ideas.

If your goal is to build your blog or your career as an author, you may get some good exposure by writing for a magazine, but in my personal experience publishing in the top magazines has done next to nothing for my career. My journalist friend mentioned to me that she has noticed the same trend since people just read the stories and rarely note the by-lines. It will be far more sustainable to build an email list, start a podcast, or host discussions in a Facebook group if you want to build a career as an author.

I have found that the best thing for my professional life and for my soul is to focus on the types of work that are within my skill sets and help me reach my goals without draining my time. I'm not a reporter who relishes the chance to interview people. I want to sit in a cafe with my headphones on and to be left alone while I work. I also want a bit more control over my writing, and book publishing provides that.

Nevertheless, there is money to be made in writing for publications, even if they appear to be vanishing more rapidly than they appear. In addition, if you simply want to publish your work in a high quality journal, you certainly have plenty of options. One of the nice aspects about writing for a magazine or journal is that rejection is often a really good sign. It means they at least replied to you. That doesn't always happen with magazines or journals! If they give you any feedback at all, that is most likely an invitation to try again. You may even find that the rejection from magazine editors will prepare you to handle the far more critical reviews that will come from book readers or blog commenters!

Bad Book Reviews

I'll be the first to admit that I tended to write critical reviews of books until I started publishing my own. I'm picky--about lots of things--especially when it comes to books. When I moved to the receiving end of reviews, I began to repent of my critical spirit toward authors, even the ones who picked deceptive titles for their books. Now that I have quite a few books available, I've done my best to avoid reading the reviews, but on the occasions when I've noticed a critical review, it can be discouraging to read a review that picks apart my book, misunderstands my intentions, or assumes the worst about me. The toughest reviews are the critical ones that I suspect to be accurate. Perhaps a reviewer picks up on an oversight I've made, or a reviewer points out a section of a chapter that I've already been insecure over. Even if there are 50 reviews that are mostly positively, the negative reviews have a way of sticking with us.

If you're concerned about receiving critical reviews (what writer isn't concerned about this?), then you have the most compelling reason to work harder on the early stages of your book. Find a few people who can give feedback on the early drafts, hire a legit editor (Hello there!), and sound out your book with a few beta readers. If you've been balking at the thought of investing in an experienced editor, think of two things. First of all, think about how it may feel to get a one or two star review. In fact, I'll help you out with that: it will feel terrible to see a book you've invested hours and hours of time into get awful reviews because you cut corners or didn't want to spend money on making your book better. Secondly, if money is a concern, get creative. Perhaps you have a skill or talent you can swap with an editor. If you have a friend who is working on a similar kind of book, you could serve as editors to each other--a competent friend is better than no editor, even if an experienced editor will provide the kind of help you really need.

Critical reviews will come no matter how hard you work. My main concern is to help you meet critical feedback with courage and a healthy sense of perspective. If you look at best-selling books or classics that show up on online retail sites, you'll notice that even the "best" books in each genre have negative reviews. You can't please everyone. Authors have to write for an audience and then understand that sometimes people outside their audience will try their book out and give it a thumbs down. In addition, some people in their audience simply won't resonate with their books.

No matter how hard I try to avoid the reviews of my books on retail sites, I can't help reading the reviews in magazines or popular websites. When I read these reviews, I try to keep in mind that not all reviews or reviewers are created equal. Sometimes reviewers either jump to conclusions or read your book through their own agendas.

For instance, one of my books was reviewed on a popular website by a theology professor from a theological tradition completely different from my own. The negative points of his review really annoyed me. While he praised certain aspects of the project, most of his criticisms were based on his disagreement with the aims laid out in the book. At the end of the day, he wanted us to write a different book. The bias of his own tradition and the types of books authors in his own tradition write prevented him from seeing our book's goal. He didn't think books like ours should even be written and published in the first place!

While blog reviews are generally on the decline as a key publicity tool for authors, there's also the possibility that a blogger or journalist could post a negative or critical review of your book. These can particularly sting because comments may begin piling up below a critical post in agreement or attacking your character. I remember one reviewer of my first book who ranted that I was a Protestant who wanted to be Catholic and people piled on in the comments about what a heretic I was. The truth is that I had a very, very negative experience growing up as a Catholic and went through a time when I hated all things Catholic with a passion. My book was committed to charitable dialogue with all Christian traditions, so I forced myself to engage with even the Catholics in a positive light. It nearly killed me at the time, but since then I've found some Catholic authors to be truly refreshing and insightful and have made friends with several practicing Catholics. As for that blog post, I had a good laugh about it and left a comment with a bit more information about my background.

Having said that, it's rarely productive to comment on critical blog posts and reviews of your books. It usually results in an endless back and forth that tends to encourage the more vindictive commenters to double down and pile on the vitriol. In the case of reviews in particular, you need to treat them as a closed case. While it may be tragic that a reviewer missed the point of your book or trashed it unfairly, move on as fast as you can. Such reviews really are inevitable, and you only make yourself appear petty and combative if you can't leave a bad review alone.

If you do want to reply to a critical blog post about you or your book, avoid replying immediately after you read the post. Give yourself a few hours to digest it and to filter your thoughts a bit. Consulting a friend will help normalize your thoughts as you consider a response. Try to avoid getting too emotional in your response and stick to simple facts as much as possible, offering details such as your intentions with the book, the story behind it, or what you've based your book on. Most importantly, post your comment, turn off any notifications for follow up replies, and leave it there. There's a 0.01% chance that further follow up will offer more clarity or change anyone's mind who disagrees with your main point. If you do continue to follow up, there's a 99.99% chance you'll get sucked into a never-ending debate where all involved parties will repeat themselves over and over again. Of course you can save yourself from all of this by simply letting the critical blog post go. Call up a friend, speak your mind in a private or secret Facebook group, or open a document on your computer and let the reviewer have it.

I honestly have never regretted letting a critical review go. The less I engage with it, the faster I'll forget it and move on with my life.

While bad reviews are a problem for many writers, most new writers have a completely different problem: no reviews or sparse reviews. In fact, whether you blog or write books, you may have a hard time convincing anyone to even look at your work. It can be especially discouraging to see your work languishing in obscurity, and once you begin spiraling in negativity, it's hard to know how to break out of it. Let's take a look at what you can do about a low number of readers.

Low Numbers of Readers

The most common complaint I hear from discouraged writers is that their sales numbers or blog readers are abysmally small. I've known this struggle too.

Aside from a critical review or comment, low sales numbers for your books or rock bottom page views for your website are some of the most soul-crushing aspects of writing. However nonchalant some of the more successful writers may seem about these numbers, we all crave to be read. Writers hope that their writing is useful as entertainment or valuable as a source of information.

While every successful writer needs to learn some basic guidelines about presenting their work, craft, editing, and publicity, I still believe that, at the end of the day, the best writing will be seen and appreciated even if that's a relatively small group. The best writing won't necessarily be the most popular writing--hello best-selling poorly written erotica. However, readers are looking for competent writers, and if you stick with it long enough, you will find some committed readers who may even share your work with others. We'll talk a bit more about publicity and marketing later, but for now, I want to focus on developing something worth reading and sharing so that you can take pride in the quality of your work.

When I started out as a full time freelancer, I made a ton of mistakes, but I at least did two things right: I wrote constantly and I read a lot of books, including books, magazines, and websites about becoming a better writer. I still do. Having written thousands of words every week and learning about the craft and business of writing gave me a foundation that I'm so grateful to have. It takes time to build up this experience and knowledge, but the best part is that you can do this. It's not like there's a secret passcode to read *Bird by Bird* or *On Writing*. *Writer's Digest* isn't hidden inside the crater of a volcano. Whether or not you have a lot of readers, you can still invest in yourself as a writer and keep practicing. Of course if you get better at writing, that doesn't guarantee that you'll find a regular audience of readers!

The investment you've made in a book or blog is important. You want a return for that work. If your writing really is a ministry, then it's fair and healthy to want that ministry to have an impact. The problem is that we can confuse lots of sales with actually helping people. You'll know you've helped people if they write notes, leave positive reviews, or post about your book on social media. However, if only a few people have been reached through your book or blog, it's worth asking whether you may have a greater ministry reach through another format or another means altogether.

If your goal is to publish commercially, poor sales on a book project could make a future in that industry difficult or impossible. Too many authors enter into publishing without any concrete ideas for selling their books or they rely on limited advice, advice that doesn't fit them or their books, or advice that is just flat out wrong. They trust the publisher to tell them what to do, but they don't realize publishers are hardly in agreement on the best ways to sell books. Some still believe that social media holds the key to selling books, while others are still setting up radio interviews for their authors. Others look down on both approaches and try to adapt as they go.

Whether you're working on a book, a series of articles, or a blog post, it can be dispiriting to see an indifferent response to your writing. I've had some of my toughest questions about my calling and gifts when a book struggles or my blog doesn't attract readers. Am I just failing to do certain things well on a professional level, or is there a deeper spiritual issue related to God's direction and calling I need to decipher?

Bad sales don't necessarily mean you should give up--at least give up as a writer. While it's possible that some people may find other methods of communicating more palatable (such as podcasting or making videos), you should begin with a bit of a reality check for your writing work. For starters, many, many authors start out with struggling websites and books that don't sell well. Do you need to stick with it and keep building? Do you need to explore another project or another angle? Do you need to improve your credentials? Are there ways to connect with readers that you haven't tried yet?

I've heard from successful bloggers and authors that they made plenty of mistakes and hit failure quite a bit when they first started out. Over time they changed their websites completely, worked on some new projects that improved their credentials and reached new readers, and altered how they spent their time each day so that they could focus on the aspects of writing they enjoyed the most. Even when you experience a little success as a writer, you'll have to change and adapt to meet the new challenges that come your way. The practices and skills that helped you succeed at first may not be sustainable forever. So it's not just the new writers that need to adapt and try new things. Even experienced writers have to do this!

If you see writing as a calling from God or even something you're pursuing as a ministry, do your best to draw a line between your identity before God and the popularity of your projects. For instance, my independent publishing projects have sold thousands more copies than my commercial publishing projects. I spent years wanting validation through commercial publishing success, but for some reason my own projects have always outperformed the commercial ones. I had directly tied my calling to write with a particular type of writing--the kind that comes with book deals, advances, editors, and publicists. When I finally accepted that my calling to write isn't necessarily tied to getting a book deal, even if editors were still asking me to pitch project ideas, I found a lot of freedom and joy by focusing on independent publishing. There's no escaping the validation that comes from better sales numbers. We'll always end up thinking we've done something right if the sales can back it up. Most of the time, that may be true-- unless you're an evil genius marketer or have insanely good connections who sell your books for you. Higher numbers of readers can certainly be a good thing for writers. That just shouldn't be the only thing we focus on. If our numbers are low, we shouldn't necessarily give up.

A difficult season as a writer is an opportunity to dig a little deeper into what you're writing about. For instance, what keeps you awake at night? What do you keep thinking about or solving? What happens when you pray about your writing or personal calling? What do trusted spiritual advisors, friends, or family members say when you share these dreams with them?

As you attempt to iron out your personal focus, take some time to look at the means you've been pursuing to get those ideas out. Are you presenting your work professionally? Are you pursuing the best avenue for your blog if you're not reaching readers? Should you spend a little more time reading about publishing or working with an editor before pursing a book project?

While the quality of your writing is extremely important, sometimes a poor presentation of your work and of yourself can stop readers before they get to even the first sentence. A poorly designed website or book can be extremely distracting to readers. Bad color choices, out of focus images, a bio that fails to convey who you are, small font, or unreadable fonts can detract from your writing. There are enough website templates, website designers, and book cover designers around that you can solve these problems quickly. You don't need to have the best website or book design, but it needs to be clean, readable, and at the very least "unnoticeable" in the sense that it won't distract readers. I've clicked away from so many websites because the design just looked awful, the font was too small, or the information I wanted, such as a person's Twitter handle, too hard to find. Even self-published books that lack proper justification can be difficult to read. You don't always notice good design until you encounter someone who hasn't used it. Of course a tweak to your design or presentation can't fix a need to change what you write about.

I've made several major shifts since I started blogging over ten years ago. For instance, my blog struggled to build a regular number of readers until I started a guest posting series every Friday for a year. My readers would skyrocket and plummet from week to week, but once I implemented this series, I created a bond with a certain group of readers who looked for my posts on a more regular basis. The series, which shared stories of women in ministry, also inadvertently helped me focus on the types of people who would be most likely to identify with my writing topics.

A few years later, I felt like my blog was stuck. I struggled to think of ideas and most of the page views were coming in for older posts. Following the lead of several friends, I stopped posting at my blog and re-launched a personal blog with a slightly different focus. It took a year to gain traction at the new site, but the shift finally unlocked several areas I'd been wanting to explore on my old site but felt unable to test out. The new site gave me the freedom I needed to launch new series for myself and guest bloggers. I also started to write longer 2,000 to 3,000 word posts that used my particular gifts better than the traditional 500-800 word posts that people have come to expect from bloggers.

Over and over again, I've learned that there's no shame in trying something new. Sometimes we fear the appearance of failure that we end up digging ourselves into deeper holes that make the sense of failure greater and greater. At a certain point we don't just fear failure. We lose hope.

If you've struggled to reach readers and you're considering a new project or a new strategy for your writing, you're not the exception. It may feel awful to raise the white flag. You may have a lingering sense of failure. I get that. I've been there. I've had conversations with friends where I forced myself to frankly say, "I'm giving up on something." The pain is real, and if anything, it indicates that you've given the best of yourself to something. You didn't approach your writing work half-heartedly, and you owe yourself some time to mourn and process that disappointment.

There's freedom on the other side of that pain. You'll heal and take another step forward. You'll have new experiences and knowledge that will make you wiser. You can keep going. No one has the power to tell you whether you should or shouldn't write. A low number of readers may offer a clue that something needs to change, but your core identity doesn't come from the outside. You can always sit down again the next day and start writing.

Growing Stronger

There's no getting away from the fear of failure, negative responses to your work, or rejection letters if you're going to continue writing for the long term. Rejection can be a terrible trial, but it can also prove extremely helpful for your soul. The rejection you face as a writer will force you to either live in misery or to find your soul's true rest in Christ. Any success you experience will fade with time, so the only real options you'll eventually face boil down to disappointment in the counterfeit identity you've created as a successful writer or your real identity before God. Some people may be clever or distracted enough to avoid facing this reality, but every writer must struggle with internal and external sources of validation.

Rejection and adversity will most certainly make you stronger because you have to face the hard facts of writing: every career and calling has bad days, and you have to decide if you're committed to this career and calling enough to endure those bad days. Too many people pursue writing because it's "neat" or a "dream" to publish a book or to see their names in print. They look ahead to the pay off and fail to take account of the daily grind and many setbacks that inevitably come up along the way.

Like many writers who have gone before me, I've taken my share of punches and have had to stagger back onto my feet. The punches will keep coming, but you do get better at expecting them, absorbing them, and bouncing back. Perhaps the most important thing you can learn about writing is that you CAN bounce back after taking a punch.

I'm most likely to bounce back from a difficult season if I have other writers and friends around me who can share in my frustrations and disappointments. I have found that it's really valuable to gain perspective from people who are writers and people who are not. The former can truly commiserate and offer some constructive feedback. The later can help you keep the big picture in mind and help you see beyond the confines of your writing world.

When it comes to your writing colleagues, share your struggles and adversity with people you trust to tell you the truth. You really don't want people to spare your feelings while telling you to publish or promote something that is terrible! Honest, constructive feedback is your greatest guard against indifferent readers and negative reviews. Constructive feedback from colleagues will also help balance out your own inner voice.

When I started out, I wasn't prepared for the long slog of learning how to write better and to build a larger audience of readers. At the same time, I see my friends who are suffocating under the weight of their own criticism, and I'm much better positioned to offer them encouragement. My sunshine optimism is both my greatest strength and my greatest weakness, and it can be balanced out when I connect with someone who may have a more critical eye but perhaps needs to lighten up a bit.

As you grow stronger and more confident with a network of fellow writers around you, there's still no escaping the fact that writing truly is a leap of faith. You can test out a book or a blog post on a group of early readers, but you simply can't predict how a piece will be received by the majority of readers. Will they love it? Will they review it? Will they share it? You can't predict these things. For all of the toughening up you need to do as a writer, you also need to hold these hopes and dreams with an open hand. Once you set your writing free in this great big world, you have to trust that your work will stand on its own merit.

Mind you, of course you can work to promote your book and develop some ways to connect with readers that are better than others. We're not completely powerless. However, so many things remain out of your control as a writer once you're done the work. It's not a simple matter of cause and effect with guaranteed outcomes for everything you do. You may find that your very best work remains largely unread, while something you cranked out with far less care becomes your most popular work ever.

Don't expect the fear of failure to go away. You'll

usually get better at facing it and you'll have better ways to counter it. Feeling a little overwhelmed may be a really good thing. It may be the sign that you're doing something big and important. If you feel a little over your head, then perhaps you're living by faith and trusting God to care for your soul along the way.

CHAPTER 3

WRITING THAT SERVES GOD AND MONEY?

Money's Impact on Spirituality

Unless you are certain you can sell around a hundred books every day or you plan to go into high stakes copywriting or some form of business writing such as writing white papers and business plans, new writers will most likely struggle to earn a sustainable income, let alone enough money to support a family for the long term. Whether you end up with too much money, too little money, or too much time spent pursuing money, money can also wreak havoc on your faith, as it can divide your loyalties and lead to all sorts of questions about how and when God provides for those who live by faith. There's certainly nothing wrong with a writer of faith working hard in order to make a living just like any other job, but if you're new to freelancing or book publishing, you may be surprised by how quickly your faith will be tested through seasons of uncertainty and sparse pay checks. In addition, writers who see their writing as a ministry have struggled to keep a healthy balance if they transition to paid writing work.

The ambition and stress associated with earning more money through writing can drag down your spirit and make it hard to keep your priorities in focus. I've noticed time and time again that I can struggle to truly enjoy time with my family when I know that we're in a perilous place financially. I begin thinking about ways to increase my income in the short term and a baseline of anxiety leaves me worried and on-edge.

When I'm worried about landing a book contract, meeting sales goals, drumming up more clients, following up on invoices, or finding more magazines or blogs to pitch, I begin to lose sight of prayer and sitting before God with scripture. In fact, it becomes hard to sit still or to have a quiet mind unless I'm sitting still to work on the next thing. There may well be seasons of crisis that require all hands of deck and some sacrifices to help make ends meet, but the long term goal is find a balance where we can prioritize prayer, time with family, and personal restoration--just to name a few of the big ones--while still getting our most important work done. Constantly compromising on our family, personal health, or prayer life is how we'll end up with damaged relationships, burn out, and a sense of alienation from God.

In my own case and in the case of many other Christian writers I know, our "work" as writers also overlaps with ministry. So while we need to set aside time to focus solely on prayer and other times to focus solely on writing, the results of the two times tend to intersect or at least support each other. One commenter on my former theology blog took great offense at the thought that I, a "Christian writer," have a "For Hire" page on my website offering editing and website content. While this commenter is an extreme example and I took great delight in deleting his remark, there's an underlying uneasiness among some Christians about paying writers and other creatives for their work related to a ministry.

In one piece I wrote for *The High Calling*, a website dedicated to serving Christians in the workplace, I discussed the many conversations I've had with artists, designers, and writers who have been expected to give churches either free work or the Christian "family discount." While the work was supposed to be professional and high quality, and these churches presumably pay other contractors full price for other services, there's something about creative work that somehow screams, "Be cheap!" In some cases churches asked multiple creative professionals for free work and just chose their favorite one, leaving several designers without anything to at least add to their portfolios. If you work at a church, please never, ever do that!

Ironically, just about every Christian can rest easy at night knowing that the pastors in their churches are being paid to do ministry. However, our tune may change when it comes to creative work that is presented as a ministry as well. I assure you that very few, if any people, get into the creative fields in order to make a lot of money. The majority of book projects aren't profitable, even the ones with commercial publishers. While some have an image of the "greedy Christian author" trying to cash in on his/her ministry, those people are more of the exception than the rule. Even the best known Christian authors who secure some of the largest advances in the industry have to add public speaking just to fill in the gaps between royalty payments.

It takes a tremendous amount of time and reflection to write excellent blog posts, articles, and books. I have no problem with paying a professional writer when I need to subcontract something out or receiving payment as a professional writer for my own work. There are times when I offer my work for free or for next to nothing in order to help a friend or ministry, but there's no reason why a professional shouldn't charge a reasonable fee for his/her work. However, some writers I know simply want to share their work for free, and blogs make that extremely easy to do. Other online services let potential readers pay whatever they want for your eBook.

Perhaps the greatest spiritual battle in my own writing career took place when I struggled to make ends meet in my first two years as a freelance writer. I felt that I had tried everything that wasn't writing, and through a convergence of prayer and circumstances, I continuously felt called to keep writing. While pursuing my writing work, I unfortunately began to associate certain kinds of writing projects, certain sales numbers, and certain career goals with my calling to write. I should have seen that I wasn't cut to make a living as a magazine writer, but for over a year I tried to pay the bills through that kind of writing. It took a writer colleague I knew from blogging to snap me out of it. She had me list out every writing skill I had and pointed out that I had neglected my expertise in website writing and book editing. Her advice combined with the constant nudge from God to keep writing provided the support I needed to endure a difficult season where we often lived from paycheck to paycheck.

As I watched our dwindling finances during those years, I often asked God what the deal was. How could God point me in this direction and then let us drown in debt and bills? What should I make of the old cliché "Where God guides, God provides"? I felt like God had directed me off a cliff and left me shattered on the rocks down below.

I don't profess to understand how exactly prayer works, how each of us hear God differently, or how we can lose focus of God's direction over time, but somehow I had lost sight of some key details along the way. Once I let go of one type of writing, I immediately found new stability and peace with my work. I don't know why I went through two years of struggle, but I also earned some hard-fought lessons about what NOT to do. When I began to hit some roadblocks and barriers in my publishing career about five years later, I was ready to try something different, realigning my goals and my processes. Once again, I found new freedom and peace once I remained open to taking my writing in a different direction. The money I'd been struggling to earn also began to fall into place along the way.

I don't imagine God dangling wads of cash before me and only dipping it down when I'm doing what God wants. Rather, in my own experience, I have been seeking God's direction for my life and running those prayers past trusted people in my life to try to stay on track. It's easy to begin inserting my own plans and goals, assuming they must be part of what God is promising me. Then again, all is not lost if we endure a little adversity and learn from our mistakes.

Writing professionally for a full or part time income brings along many of the same challenges small business owners face. While you have tons of flexibility and control over your work day, goals, and type of projects you take on, you also face all of the pressure that comes with uncertain cash flow, all of the responsibility to solve problems, and all of the pitfalls that come with losing balance when you set your own work schedule. You can be as lazy or ambitious as you like. You can worry about money as much or as little as you want. You can take as much or as little vacation as you want, provided you get your work done.

Writers tend to think we'll keep a perfect balance in our lives if we control our work days and professional goals, but that isn't always the case. Sometimes we can be terrible bosses and managers for ourselves, forcing ourselves to work long hours and allowing work concerns to invading family time in the evening or weekends. If you sense a nudge from God to write and to even pursue that writing professionally as an author or as a freelancer, expect struggles, difficult seasons, tricky questions, and imbalances that need to be corrected. Let's look at some ways that writing and money can become complicated for people of faith who pursue writing as a career.

Money's Impact on Creativity

For most of us, we shouldn't become a writer JUST to make money unless the plan is to shoot for big ticket corporate copy writing. You may make some money with blogging, publishing, or freelancing. You may even make an obscene amount of money if you hit on the right topic or trend at the right time. However, if you have any personal goals that are rooted in creativity or ministry, don't let the promise of money become the engine that drives your writing work. I've heard from quite a few writers who have either struggled to make ends meet with writing or who found that the daily pressure to make money with their writing killed their creativity.

If you need money right now, polish your resume and start applying for jobs. Creating a sustainable income as a writer takes time. Any kind of writing you do is a learned skill that takes significant time to develop. In addition, it's extremely difficult to build a steady income stream without a base of clients for your freelance work or a massive marketing platform for your books.

If you really want to make money as a writer, the most sustainable path will be in the business world or marketing industry. Writers can earn a significant amount of money for their time working on white papers, writing sales pages, or writing technical copy. There are really positive elements to this kind of work too. Working on a white paper means I usually have to immerse myself in a particular business or industry and meet new people with passions that are completely different from my own. It's energizing to see a client's struggles to put something into words and to work on possible solutions. If you're particularly passionate about particular products, it may be a dream come true to write technical copy about them, as is the case for my friend who works at Apple!

Having said all of that, there are plenty of ways to make money as a writer, but it may take more time than you'd like to build your expertise and base of clients. It may even involve revenue sources that you aren't initially interested in pursuing. For instance, the majority of nonfiction authors I know make most of their money through speaking or through teaching online courses. A few have built enough of a following that publishers will give them large advances, but as their audiences and advances grow, so do their speaking invitations and other writing opportunities. In fact, if they want to meet the sales goals set by their publishers, they need to take advantage of at least a few of these events and article writing opportunities.

If you're hoping to make a sustainable long-term income in publishing alone, you need to sell a lot of books. Keep in mind that most advances these days are close to $5,000. And even if you strike it rich and land a $25,000 advance or more, that will dry up pretty fast if you don't have any other income sources (don't forget your agent gets a cut, you'll receive the advance in two payments, and then you'll have to pay taxes). If you look at the self-published or independent authors who are making a living full time by writing, you'll typically find they write genre-fiction such as science fiction, romance, mysteries, or thrillers.

Before you sit down to write seriously, take a good look at the financial side of writing. If you need to make money and you believe that writing is one of your most valuable skills, then there are paths forward. You can read blogs on copywriting, pick up top books in your industry, and take classes at local colleges to get an edge in your field. If you want to pursue book publishing or blogging as a creative outlet, ministry, and side income source, there are a lot of ways forward as well. If you work hard enough, get some breaks, and keep learning, you may even earn a substantial income. Based on what I've read, my book sales place me in the top 5-10% of published authors, and I can assure you, I've never made enough from my writing to support our family for an entire year, even if it's been an important source of financial stability for us.

If you're sitting down to write a book or to launch a blog with massive bills hanging over your head, you're starting in the worst possible place. Don't let the pressure of bills kill your creativity. It's far better to depend on writing work that pays reliably for your income and to gradually build your publishing and/or blogging profile without the threat of financial disaster looming.

For me, I have learned that sales numbers and dollars can be stress inducing and restrictive for my writing work. My writing depends on following the ideas that are most engaging and the needs of readers that are most pressing. I can't let obsessing over sales numbers dominate my writing and creative time. It's much better to let your writing income become a bonus to your existing income and to only invest in it full time when you have the financial stability to do so. In fact, a look at the type of income you can expect from book publishing may be the most important reality check for professional writers who want to build sustainable careers without wrecking their souls.

Book Publishing Revenue

If you're new to book publishing, I want you to brace yourself for a huge reality check here. The majority of authors who make a steady, somewhat respectable income from book publishing write genre fiction. High earning nonfiction authors are more of the exception than the rule. Even many of the most successful nonfiction authors I know depend on advertising revenue on their websites and speaking engagements to pay the bills since their book royalties aren't steady or significant enough. Most are in dual-income households where the dips in revenue in between book advances or book releases are leveled out by another income source.

Even some established authors with huge backlists have lamented that the rise of eBooks has led to worrying declines in annual royalty checks. And yes, you read that correctly: most commercial authors get paid annually and won't see their sales numbers until an annual report arrives in the mail. You can find exceptions to every trend, but it's not responsible to jump into publishing with the assumption that you'll earn a steady, sustainable income within a year or two.

While I certainly know of authors who have received advances in the $25,000-$50,000 range, it's far more common for first time authors to land in the $5,000 ballpark for an advance. The majority of the time these first time authors won't see more than $5,000 since their books typically struggle to earn out the advance.

Authors who are published independently (the preferred word over "self-publishing these days) or commercially will have to think of ways to continually find new readers in order to keep their sales going. Even if you're working with a publisher, your publicity push will last a few weeks. Some publishers will keep your book visible at conferences, especially if you're a speaker at that conference. For most of us, we have to develop our own networks and "connection systems" to keep putting our books in front of readers. That could be a blog, podcast, newsletter, or some combination of all three. Whether you're working with a commercial publisher who offers an advance or you're independently publishing on your own dime, I'll lay out a rough guide for book publishing that will help you understand how you could hope to make money from the process.

Generally speaking, if you're working with a commercial publisher, your viability as an author depends on earning out your advance and even surpassing a publisher's expectations. A lot of publishing experts suggest that authors work for at least two years to build up an email list, blog following, or social media group organized around your book's topic. Perhaps some authors believe that, in a perfect world, authors should just work on their books and let the publishers handle promoting the book to retailers who, in turn, sell the book to customers. I would certainly prefer that! These days the book selling process is far more complicated, with publishers taking on a limited role in promoting most books and focusing on the production, a relatively standard marketing plan, and more robust marketing pushes for their most important releases. Authors are expected to be on the front lines connecting with their readers and encouraging potential readers to make a purchase at a retailer's website or store. The pre-orders and first 2-3 weeks of a new book's release can often make or break a commercial book project.

If you want publishers to keep writing checks and providing the editorial, design, and publicity support, you need to play the game. Gather endorsements, develop ways to connect with thousands upon thousands of readers, jump on publicity opportunities, and keep thinking of ways to find new readers for you books. Honestly, if you go the independent route, it's just going to be more of the same kind of work. The main differences are: you have control over when and how much you discount your book, have zero external pressure to meet sales goals, can get real time data on any promotion (which is a HUGE benefit), and can regularly update your manuscript to include excerpts of future books and drive readers back to your personal newsletter or website in order to sell more books in the future. In other words, independent authors can use what publicist Tim Grahl calls the "long game" approach to publicity. While a big sales spike during your book's first two weeks will help immensely, each author can decide how much pressure to apply during a book's launch.

Whether you're working with a large publisher or you're independently publishing, the one starting point for making money off a book is to get the book in front of people. Every author will have a different approach to this based on his/her popularity and audience. However, every book launch involves sending free books to reviewers, fans who will spread the word, and price promotions that will spark early sales in the hopes of landing on a bestseller list somewhere. With so much focus on selling books through online retailers, reviews on leading sites such as Amazon and Goodreads are proving especially important at the point of sale. I've heard some publicists recommend aiming for at least 25 reviews, but in order to do that, you need to probably ask at least 75 people. Others have noticed that once a book has 50 reviews on Amazon, your chances of being discovered increase significantly, which means asking an additional 75 people for reviews.

We'll never know exactly what makes Amazon's algorithm promote certain books, but the basic principle remains the same for selling books: give away free copies to reviewers and sell the book at a discount, especially early on. For instance, before releasing one of my independent books, I ran a pre-sale at $.99 for a month and accumulated around 340 pre-orders since I placed two guest posts on some high traffic websites and contacted the subscribers on my email list with the promotion. That was good enough to debut at #1 for both of my book's categories. Mind you, I only made about $.35 per sale. However, that low price prompted a lot of people to take a chance on my book based simply on the premise. Once 5-star reviews started showing up from my early reviewers, I bumped the price to $1.99 for a week, and sales continued fairly strong for a few days. My royalty was only $.84 per sale at that price, but if you consider that authors tend to make around $1.20-$1.50 per paperback sale on a commercial book, and typically less for the eBook versions, it only takes two or three sales to roughly equal what I would have made with two commercial sales at regular price. Once my book built some momentum, I raised the price to $2.99 and steady sales continued in the months that followed.

Most authors like myself who aren't household names or don't have a massive online following will need to rely on high traffic guests posts combined with some kind of price promotion or special offer in order to get noticed. Perhaps an unknown author has the credentials or experience that will prompt readers to take a chance on his/her book at full price. However, independent publishing does allow authors to make themselves visible through a key purchasing factor: price.

If you feel bad about selling your eBook version at a low price, keep in mind that almost every publisher now uses eBook price promotions to either jumpstart sales on their books or to rejuvenate a title from their backlists. In fact, you may have heard about recent controversies where pastors and other Christian authors have been involved in schemes where a publisher paid a "marketing company" around $250,000 to strategically purchase copies of their books nationwide in order to land a book on a bestseller list. This up front investment isn't necessarily throwing money to the wind for the sake of an author's ego, although it sometimes becomes that. The hope is that the visibility on several bestseller lists will lend credibility to a title, even if the author is well known, and generate additional sales. If a publisher is willing to invest thousands in trying to land a book on the New York Times list, it's not such a big deal to offer a price promotion to get online retailers to take notice of your title. Besides, a $.35 royalty per sale is better than obscurity!

Most importantly, price promotions provide a simple and sustainable way for authors get their work out there. Bumping your book up various bestseller lists at online retailers through a discounted price gives your book valuable visibility. In fact, I've found that the better my visibility, the more my books will sell on their own. This is the goal that many authors work toward. As we gradually, and hopefully sustainably, build our audiences through our own means (this could include in-person events, blog subscribers, email subscribers, social media, or writing for high profile websites), we can use price promotions to keep our books in front of readers on bestseller lists for our respective categories.

While a $.99, $1.99, or $2.99 price promotion can make

an author like myself who isn't a household name easier to discover at online retailers, different versions of this strategy are used depending on the author. For instance, take blogging superstar Jessica Turner who released her book *The Fringe Hours* on several bestsellers lists by offering several different price promotions. In most cases the book wasn't close to $.99, but her book was in strong enough demand that even a 30%, 40%, 50% limited time discount was enough to put readers over the edge. Her 50% print pre-order sale at Barnes and Noble was especially powerful for getting her book noticed on social media. In the lead up to her release, she continued to send special offers, giveaways, and contests to her readers as ways to prompt pre-orders. While the tactics were different, the same big picture strategy still applied: drive readers to pre-order your book before it's released with a price promotion and your chances of being discovered by new readers will increase since your book will show up on various bestseller lists.

There's a long view to keep in mind when it comes to making your commercial or independent publishing career financially sustainable. Perhaps some are encouraged to know there are ways for a relatively unknown writer to connect with readers, while others are horrified by all of the marketing, sales, and price promotion ideas they need to consider in order to publish books. I want you to be empowered to take control of your publishing career, but of course the last thing I want is for you to think that this is all about the money. I mean, heck, I'm suggesting price promotions after all! Most authors I know aren't interested in becoming social media superstars or mastering the finer points of SEO for their blogs. They don't want to tour the country on speaking tours at glitzy events, and they wouldn't even know how to get involved in that if they could. They don't want to spend their days marketing their books because they care so deeply about the writing process. Most importantly, they fear that building a massive following could be bad for their souls, but they also would like to still sell copies of their books to make their work sustainable.

I have generally found that earning too much money isn't a problem for most writers. Even the writers I know who have received large advances received them in smaller installments that stretched out over time, keeping them from ever feeling flush. My more successful independent books have done much the same for me. If anything, our souls can suffer if we obsessively check out online sales rankings at various retailers. While you should certainly check a ranking in order to see if a particular promotion or pricing strategy has worked or if a new promotion is needed, it's all too easy to start associating your self worth with a sales rank. Many authors share that checking a sales rank can be crushing for their souls. The more I've thought about marketing, such as buying an ad on an eBook discount site, listing my book with a Twitter site that shares promotions, or picking up an ad on Facebook to share a limited time discount, the less damage a sales rank does to my soul. If I'm simply measuring the impact of a promotion, a sales rank is just a tool that lets me know when I need to try something new or add another promotion to my to-do list.

I admit that it was hard to swallow the thought that I needed to sell my books so cheaply at first. It's also disconcerting at times to realize how much time you need to invest on the front end of your career to the work of promotion and marketing. While your craft comes first, you really do need to look at your options for promotion in order to understand what you should invest in. The last thing you want to do is waste your time on something that isn't your first priority to begin with. In fact, my goal for myself and for you is to spend the vast majority of each day writing. Most of my promotional work is either tied to my book writing work, such as blogging about future book ideas or emailing my newsletter readers about my latest project, or calls for minimal time, such as buying an ad on Facebook. While you will need to learn some best practices in order to use a tool like Facebook ads well, the long term goal is to learn some basic skills, focus on writing, and then run ads when you need them or can afford them. If you find that you really struggle with keeping track of your sales and sales rank each day in order to run an ad campaign, then focus on building a newsletter and just writing notes to your readers to keep them informed about your latest progress. If you enjoy the chatter of social media or have a knack for designing images for quotes, then focus your time on building that.

Whether you publish commercially or independently, you will have to learn more about marketing and publicity than you would ever want to know. I confess that I have struggled in this area. I really only want to write books, but as I've learned what I like to do and what I don't like doing, I've been able to focus on the marketing strategies and tactics that make the most sense to me and that appear to be most effective. Besides, as I work on building my own publishing plans for the future, I can rely on my freelance writing income to help make ends meet when my publishing income falls short of providing what our family needs.

Freelancing Revenue

I'm often asked how to build a freelance writing business, and these days I've talked to enough freelancers to know that there are many different ways to get started. Some build networks through classes, conferences, and local business events. Some advertise, while others fight and claw for work through online job boards. Others build strong websites that have excellent Search Engine Optimization and even combine that with listings on job sites like LinkedIn or ThumbTack. I've done some combination of all of the above, but I have definitely found the most work by simply making my services and experience clear on my website and getting work from people who already knew about me. Just as you wouldn't slap together a resume for a job interview, you can't afford to build a base of freelance clients if your website is a disorganized, unprofessional mess. Some studies have also shown that a professional website can dramatically improve how visitor's perceive your abilities even if you're just starting out. If you "look" like a pro, people are more likely to treat you like on.

I encourage you to begin with a focused "For Hire" page on your website. If you really want to get it noticed, link to it prominently on all of your key online networks, such as your Twitter profile, Facebook page, and blog. Use keywords that potential clients may use. For instance, I've gotten several clients simply because they searched for writers and editors in my city. Apparently I was the only website that showed up because I mentioned my city on several pages throughout my site! Focus on a few things you do really well and make sure they show up as keywords high up on your For Hire page.

If you're brand new to freelancing, I strongly encourage working on a few pro bono projects at the beginning. There are a bunch of things that can go wrong while working with a client, and I've made plenty of mistakes along the way. For instance, it can be quite difficult to help a client determine what he/she wants out of a website. Most professional companies have extensive forms their clients have to fill out and an extensive review process.

When I started out, I had a 5-question form that a client filled out along with a few email chats to guide my website write up. While I'm pretty sure I wrote what he asked for, he was not happy with it. In fact, he only responded with, "This is shitty." We parted ways after that, and I have since learned that the planning process for writing a website from scratch takes way more than a few questions. Based on subsequent clients, I'm fairly certain that I had failed to help this website owner distill what he wanted his website to do.

Before I took up author coaching as a source of income, I had spent a number of years helping friends and colleagues sort out the challenges of book publishing. I began to recognize a kind of rhythm to the ups and downs of book writing. By the time I took on brand new authors who were often overwhelmed with the challenges facing them, I had significant experience guiding my friends through each step of the way, to say nothing of navigating them through relationships with a wide variety of publishers. Although you can certainly fake expertise on a few occasions, lack of experience will most certainly come back to bite you with clients. You may fail to understand a client's needs, fail to present a clear contract, fail to secure a down payment, fail to specify what happens when a payment is late, or fail to provide a service that is adequate for his/her needs. By picking up some pro bono work you'll get some experience and work out the kinks before a big check is hanging in the balance.

While I'm certainly open to working directly with clients for a freelance website or newsletter copywriting, I've learned that I thrive best when partnering with a company or individual who provides writing services or website design and allows me to essentially work as a subcontractor. Yes, the payments are lower than if I managed the process myself, but I personally thrive when

I'm handed a project to do and that's where my responsibility ends.

I also highly recommend posting at least a few advertisements on sites like Craig's List if you're just getting started. You never know what will come of a conversation with a potential client. I've found that there are two traps to avoid: people who think you can do more than you're able because they assume a "writer" can handle ANY type of writing job and people who offer far less than you're worth because "anyone" can write something. Keep your listing brief and specific. Only take on the clients who contact you about the type of work you know you can accomplish effectively. In addition, set your prices according to a third party guide in order to minimize disputes over your rates. For instance, *Writer's Digest* usually has a chart each year right in the beginning that offers low, middle, and high prices for each writing service. If you're just starting out, it's OK to set your price low, but keep in mind that your location may also play a role in determining what's a "low" price. A low price in New York and Washington D.C. could be much higher than the low price in a small Midwestern city.

Whether you pursue large projects such as ghost writing or writing white papers for companies, or smaller projects such as blogging for businesses or writing articles, continue to pursue multiple revenue sources. If you're relying on one client for the majority of your income, you're in a particularly vulnerable place since writers are generally viewed as replaceable. I have seen time and time again that businesses view their marketing budget as expendable, and if you're particularly successful, you may actually be most vulnerable to cuts since some businesses may believe the gains you've made will remain without the attention and expertise you provide.

For instance, I once built excellent search engine traffic

for a client's website around certain keywords, but after several years they cut me loose and turned their blog over to someone on staff who didn't have a blogging background. I can't say whether that was the right choice for them at the time, but after five months they brought me back. Thankfully I had several other regular clients and more than enough work when the bad news arrived.

As work comes and goes, I have to drum up new business, getting referrals, recommendations, or posting a bit more frequently about the editing and writing services I offer. I also make a point of never admitting to a client that I have "loads and loads of free time" if that's ever the case. Keep the details of your business close to your chest. Be flexible by all means with setting up a meeting, but don't make it sound like you're starved for work and really desperate to meet! In fact, it's best to continue seeking new clients even when you're busy. When it comes to creative work, it's wise to have a bunch of prospective clients in the pipeline. Oftentimes clients tell me they need to hire me a few months before they're ready to work, and more than a few clients disappeared after asking for a price quote and saying they'd be in touch any day. I never want to feel like I need to bug prospective clients for work right when an existing client drops me.

I have generally found most freelance writing job boards to be a waste of time. Even if I do land a project with a potential client through a job listing board, many are looking for the cheapest rate possible rather than developing a long-term working relationship and paying a living wage. Whether you've been friends with someone for years or you've just connected over email, always set up a basic working agreement, including a partial payment up front for larger projects. Develop set policies that are uniform for every client, then you won't have the awkward situations, as I have had, where you do hours and hours of work for a friend who drops off right before the project ends and never pays a dime. If I had at least insisted on him paying half up front, I would have gotten something for the considerable time I spent on his project. We often think that developing a contract with a friend will be awkward, but it's actually far worse to do work for a friend who never pays!

Speaking of friends who don't pay, let's take a moment to talk a bit more about working for churches and religious groups. There's a tendency among Christians to consider working for each other a "family affair." It's not uncommon for creative professionals to be asked to work for free, at a steep discount, or without a contract. While there's always room for a little pro bono work or volunteering within extremely specific confines, every church or Christian ministry project should have a contract with clear terms. While I'm sympathetic with cash-strapped churches, cash-strapped writers shouldn't necessarily feel compelled to give churches a steep discount for professional work.

The client doesn't determine whether your work is ministry. Your mindset before God determines whether your work is ministry. God has given you specific gifts and talents that you can use to serve others. We don't ask pastors to go off the clock in order to "minister" to us. However, once we talk about creative work in the church, some seem to think that money suddenly undermines one's ability to minister or to serve God

I encourage you to prayerfully consider ways you can be generous, but don't let a church project put you in financial jeopardy. While there are some excellent church leaders who treat their staff and contractors really well, there are also some church leaders who lack professional experience and may not plan on honoring a contract's terms or respecting your limitations as a professional. Hopefully those cases are few and far between. However, if you bring up this topic with a group of Christian writers, designers, and music producers, you'll usually hear stories about churches, religious leaders, and Christian businesses with broken contracts and unpaid invoices. To make things worse, even a contract will not protect a writer. Who wants to be the guy who sues a church or who makes waves about a dishonest pastor? If you know how these things usually play out in churches, you can probably already hear people saying, "Not our pastor! He would never do that!" In some cases it's more trouble than it's worth to demand accountability from a Christian organization.

Having said all of that, freelancers face these sorts of challenges in any setting. It's just that the Christian world adds some new challenges since Christians aren't supposed to sue each other and should resolve all conflicts among ourselves. If only Paul had commanded one of his churches to pay for the services they received from a contractor! Freelancers need just one proof text. Is that too much to ask?

Your best defense against being exploited in a Christian or non-Christian setting is to clearly define the nature of the work and the payment terms in a mutually agreed upon contract. Ask your client to fill out several detailed forms specifying what they want and include a payment schedule that identifies a specific point person responsible for sending your payment. Don't fall victim to disorganized committees, volunteer bookkeepers, or pastors who may drop the ball during their busy weeks. Multiple meetings with the point people on staff ensure any confusion is resolved, and a written project plan allows the client to clearly state expectations and goals. Free consultations take time, but stop looking at the time you're losing and think of how bad things could be if you create something your client hates or that never gets paid! You could spend many more hours working on something that never even brings in a single dollar.

Article Revenue

Writing blog posts and magazine articles for revenue has advantages and disadvantages for freelance writers. On the one hand, you can earn a great hourly wage and reach a ton of readers if you write for a top site or outlet. On the other hand, writing for a magazine can be time-consuming if you're pitching articles to an editor who doesn't know you or if you're new to magazine writing. In addition, very few blogs pay their contributors, with even the top outlets offering some mixture of exposure or shared advertising revenue--the latter is only profitable for the top tier writers in most cases.

The number of high paying magazine opportunities has declined in recent years, and if you're just starting out as a freelancer, I don't recommend writing for magazines or websites as a steady source of income. It can be a supplemental source of income, but it will take time to learn how to query editors effectively, to write articles according to extremely specific guidelines and audiences, and to build enough trust with an editor that he/she will begin to seek you out for projects. However, if an editor at a major publication begins to rely on you, that may result in a steady stream of work and lead to additional opportunities for other publications in the same niche.

When it comes to writers hoping to publish commercially, if you're seeking to develop a connection with an audience for your book project, it can be extremely hard to convert magazine readers into book buyers. Agents and editors may want to see that you've published in some popular magazines, but those articles will not necessarily turn into book sales. The main benefit is to demonstrate a professional writing history. Even if you publish a post on a magazine website with lots of traffic on a topic related to your book, there's no guarantee that those readers will follow you or buy your book in large enough numbers to justify the work you've put into your article. You may convert more readers into buyers, social media followers, or blog subscribers if you write for a higher traffic blog in your niche where the blogger in charge may allow you more control over your by-line and toss in a call to action at the end of your post. The path you choose just depends on your goals: immediate income or audience-building for future book sales.

It's also difficult to write for magazines as a source of income because articles can be cut down or cancelled due to changes at a magazine. I had placed an article in a top regional magazine that paid by the word and spent a significant amount of time on the article. By the time the article published (a year after submission, no less), my article, which was paid by the word, had been cut down to a third of its original length. The check, which arrived thirty days after publication, was much smaller than anticipated!

If you want to earn direct and reliable income by writing for magazines or journals, begin with one of two (if not both) general guidelines:

1. Write for magazines or journals you're already reading or interested in reading.

2. Write for magazines or journals with a trade focus in your niche.

If you aren't reading a magazine already, it will be much harder to match the voice and style the magazine wants. You won't be familiar with the needs they're trying to address, and you will struggle to break in. If you're already reading a magazine, you can look up its contributor guidelines and find ways to break in, such as writing sidebar content. When you pitch an editor, demonstrate that you're already familiar with their work by matching your pitch to existing articles. I always pitch editors with two very short ideas just to increase the odds of being accepted. You can also reach out on social media, asking editors if they're looking for anything in particular at this time or if there's a preferred way to pitch articles to them. Rather than lamenting the fact that editors rarely respond to pitches, think of ways you can make an editor's job easier. They're often on tight deadlines, trying to make articles by a variety of writers fit the tone of their publication. Editors will always need flexible writers who understand their magazines.

While you can make the most money by writing for the widest audience, new freelancers will find the most success in the trade market where readership is smaller but also more stable. Think of it this way, many companies pay for trade magazines in order to stay informed on current trends, so they view the subscription as a cost of doing business rather than a luxury expense, which is a major challenge that publications with wider audiences face. Trade publications are often seeking articles that are either extremely practical or extremely specific with industry insight, and those types of articles can be easier to research and write, compared to a broader magazine that wants a catchy angle or provocative perspective. You don't necessarily need "pop" or "sizzle" to write in this market. Once you've proven yourself to an editor at a trade magazine, you may also get repeat business more frequently.

There are no sure things in the writing business, but if you want to write short-form content in order to make a steady income or to build your career as an author, magazine writing isn't necessarily the best path forward.

While every author is different, you may find more success in building a marketing platform by creating a personal or community blog and then growing your subscribers by writing for online magazines or popular, high traffic blogs. Once you've built a blog, you have many different ways to earn a stable income.

Blog Revenue

Most of the bloggers I know start writing because of either a creative passion to share their writing with a wider audience or a desire to fill a need among a niche of readers. In fact, I can't think of a single blogger, especially bloggers who write about their faith, who started a blog in order to make money. If anything, the most successful bloggers included ads as their sites grew and took up more of their time. By including ads they covered their hosting fees and at least paid them for part of their time spent writing and managing their sites. Personally speaking, I started blogging as a creative outlet, never considering that it could help earn money through ads or help catch a publisher's eye.

I didn't know what to do with myself when I finished seminary, and about a month after my last class ended, my friend emailed me with a link, a user name, and a password to a blog. He had set the whole thing up as a way to keep our conversations about God going. He posted a few times in the early days, but I felt like I'd been waiting all of my life to start blogging. The short format and immediacy of posting was ideal at that point in my life.

I spent the first few years blathering on about church and theology without much direction. I wasn't really saying anything all that new. I was one of many deconstructing the struggles of my faith and my inability to fit in at church. It took me far too long to start piecing together the ways I could write posts that were actually unique and in something resembling my own voice. Over time my audience finally grew to the point that I considered attempting some ads on my blog.

When I started blogging in 2005, it was extremely bad form for Christian bloggers to advertise in their sidebars. We didn't have Twitter accounts where we could post ads, and the thought of a sponsored post was completely anathema (Can you imagine a sponsored post about "Testamints" or the latest Patriot's Bible?). Since then, ads, sponsored posts, and sponsored tweets are fairly common on blogs these days for better or worse. Sometimes bloggers note which posts are sponsored, and sometimes they don't disclose it.

The biggest difference these days is that more distinctly faith-based advertising networks and causes exist for Christian blogs than in the early 2000's. The advertising networks available are far more targeted and sophisticated. When I started with my first ads, I had all kinds of crazy stuff showing up, like "singing prayer bowls" and "funeral flowers." These sorts of ads were showing up because of my blog's "religion" category. Over time new ad networks emerged with better ads that actually had a prayer of being clicked on by my readers. These ads covered all of my hosting costs and brought in a little extra cash to cover part of my coffee habit too. While some of my friends focused on posting daily and searching for the best advertising networks, I personally wasn't too invested in blog advertising. Among my many reasons, I didn't want people to click away from my blog when they visited it! These days I want visitors to sign up for my newsletter or to buy one of my books.

Speaking of buying books on a blog, an alternative to blog ads is affiliate revenue. For instance, the Amazon affiliate program offers a small percentage of every purchase that visitors to your site make when they click through a link on your site with an affiliate code and then make a purchase on Amazon. However, you receive a percentage of any product purchased when someone clicks through on your affiliate link. So a shopper who goes on to purchase a pile of books after clicking through your book's affiliate link will bring in some additional revenue. I always use affiliate links on my blog when I release a book in order to earn a little additional revenue from those who make a purchase on Amazon. Some readers want to know if your site has affiliate links, so it's often good to include a disclaimer at the end of your About page or in your footer just noting that visitors should assume some links are affiliate links.

The blogger who led the way in earning a living as a blogger is Darren Rowse of ProBlogger. Rowse set up the popular Digital Photography blog where he generates income from multiple sources, but over the years he's been a leading advocate of affiliate sales. And you can't blame him, right? Digital cameras sell for big bucks. We can imagine him posting a review of a new camera, slapping a link at the end of the post, and cracking open the champagne when he opens his affiliate statement each quarter. I'm overstating things here, but the point is that you shouldn't leave potential revenue on the table if you can simply and ethically earn it through your blog. If you're already linking to a favorite book or product, why not include your own affiliate code with a disclaimer?

If you'd rather not explore advertising or affiliate networks, you can also look into setting up your own advertising rates. Many bloggers have set up pages on their sites targeted specifically at potential advertisers. At bare minimum, they list their page views, subscribers, and social media statistics. The tough part will be setting your rates since blog advertising can be a bit like the wild west at times. Back when I sold advertising slots, I looked for blogs that were similar to my own and compared their page views and rates to my own, setting my monthly rates and placement guidelines accordingly. For instance, an ad that appears above the fold costs more than an ad further down the sidebar. I've found that both businesses and individuals reaching out for publicity on my blog have been willing at times to purchase a limited time ad block if the rate was reasonable enough for them. I've also proposed advertising blocks to certain groups.

I come from the school of thought that a blog is a great place to test out ideas, to find new freelance writing clients, and to connect with new readers. Blog revenue has always been a lower priority for me. That isn't to say you shouldn't explore affiliate programs or set up an advertising page. It could be a great way to supplement your freelance or publishing income. Just beware the temptation to post click-bait posts in order to bring in new readers to pump up your advertising revenue. This very practice has resulted in news websites chasing after sensational stories, fear-mongering, and celebrity gossip to the detriment of real reporting. We've all seen those viral posts that promise tears or amazement just 17 seconds into a particular animal video.

Some Christian bloggers have certainly fallen into the trap of chasing after the latest controversy or fallen leader in order to get additional page views either for subscribers or revenue. One well-known ministry even bought a church's email list and then sent an email promising insider knowledge about a former pastor's scandal. The church justified this shady process by claiming that the goal was to sell software that could help many Christians, but it's tough to promise redemption in one moment while dragging a fellow Christian through the mud, no matter how nefarious his actions may have been.

Social media has been a particularly powerful tool for bloggers who rely on lots of visitors, who find them via social media, to click on their advertisements and affiliate links. While Facebook pages can be unreliable, and there's no telling what Instagram, Pinterest, or Twitter will do in the future to their algorithms and user-experience, these have all provided significant amounts of traffic to blogs who then leverage that traffic for their advertising. A highly sharable image or graphic can make the rounds quickly on Pinterest and Facebook, while a widely shared tweet can build momentum. While tactics and overall strategies will change over time, it's not uncommon for bloggers to build their social media platforms with a mix of shareable images and updates and then promote their latest posts with their followers in order to get click-throughs to their blogs where readers will click on ads. In other words, my strategy of just sharing a blog post two times a day would hardly cut it in the big leagues of blog advertising. I've heard that some bloggers aim to share 20-30 social media updates a day in order to keep their readers engaged. In other words, making a living from blog advertising can become a full time job! This is all made particularly daunting by social media sites changing algorithms and terms of use that could make certain tactics irrelevant.

If you want to devise ways to make more money from your blog, there are plenty of people who can help you figure that out. If you have peace about earning advertising revenue, then it can go a long way toward helping you earn a living as a writer with integrity and a commitment to God's calling. There's no danger of compromise if you want to advertise ethical businesses on your website. I have no qualms with affiliate sales. It's my hope that you'll have a clear sense of mission for your writing work and that the work you do is directed by God's leading and not a need to make a quick buck on your blog.

If you'd rather think of a way to support yourself that doesn't rely on the volatility of social media or advertising networks, there is another option that offers more control but also promises many ways to mess up. The greater the opportunities, the greater the risks.

The Up-Sell

If you've ever signed up for a marketing company's email list, and you should just for the experience of it, you'll find that any offers of free content usually come with an "up-sell" at some point. For instance, if you sign up for HubSpot's email list, you'll usually get some great free stuff, such as social media reports, templates for PowerPoint, and tips on how to connect with more readers/customers. However, the free content isn't an end to itself. In fact, HubSpot is first and foremost a content marketing company, so if anyone can use content to market themselves, it should be HubSpot! Each free report or template includes a little invitation to join a free or paid seminar that dives deeper into the topic covered in the included content. In addition, there's usually some sort of offer along the way to try out their marketing software, which is the ultimate goal of their content marketing since repeat revenue from a loyal customer is far more reliable than a one time seminar participant.

The end goal of the free content is to generate leads for their marketing products and training events. If they just sat around giving out free reports, they wouldn't be able to stay in business! Many authors use a similar approach with their readers, using some free short eBooks or reports to gain newsletter subscribers and then selling books or bigger ticket items to their subscribers. While they hope to sell lots of books to their subscribers, they're also hoping a few of those committed readers will also purchase a related up-sell down the line that brings in more revenue.

The up-sell isn't necessarily a bad thing. In fact, it can be a natural and good thing in some cases. I know several authors with tremendous expertise and talent who give away great ideas on their blogs, sell books, and also offer courses and events that all build on each other quite naturally. In fact, if you hope to make a full time living as a writer, some kind of up-sell down the line will most likely be necessary. I've even hosted a small prayer and writing retreat that could technically be considered an up-sell, even if our profit margin was slim because we wanted to create a particular kind of experience and keep it affordable.

Having said that, I've grown a bit wary of the many new courses and seminars from authors who really don't have all that much expertise in the first place. I sign up for lots of email lists just to see what other authors and marketing experts are up to. I want to know how they communicate with readers and what they're trying to sell me. I've given quite a few side eyes when I've opened my inbox.

Still, it's definitely possible to set up a reasonable up-sell if you plan ahead and think it through. You'll need a massive network of readers, subscribers, and social media followers before you can set up a big ticket event or course. The constraints of cost, time, and calendars will immediately weed out even those who are interested in the first place, who will most likely be a small number of people to begin with.

Any kind of successful up-sell needs to offer something truly unique that potential customers can't find anywhere else. The greater your expertise, the more likely you'll find success. When I partnered with some friends to host writing retreat, we tried to offer an affordable holistic experience at a rural location with walking trails, gourmet food, spiritual direction, and discussions about particular aspects of the writing life. I can't think of anyone else who offered that. However, in retrospect, I can see that we needed a larger contact base. We kept costs low for attendees, but we still struggled to break even because our network of contacts wasn't large enough yet.

If you have a valuable skill or expertise that is related to your writing work, you can certainly lead 1-2 hour workshops on your own or through community groups. I've had a lot of success lining up publishing workshops through community centers or arts councils. The pay isn't amazing in most cases, but since I know all of the content already and have a book to sell at my events, I can build a little additional income based on work I've already completed.

In fact, as you look at ways you can earn a sustainable income as a writer, the key is to consider ways you can expand the reach of writing work you've already completed. If you've written a book, find a way to present the material in a different format to a different group. We all want to receive and process information differently, and perhaps authors get a bit too hung up on presenting their ideas in book form. Some people may prefer attending a class or online course rather than reading a book. Others may prefer to "read" your blog via a podcast. The greatest barriers for many authors may be their technology skill sets and their time available to make these other content pieces.

There's also the risk that people won't show up for your event or class--offering a rather bracing deterrent for many. I even experimented with offering an online writing community that offered coaching in a supportive group context, and I didn't get enough participants to make it cost-effective. I have since learned that most people prefer one-on-one (paid) coaching for their writing work and free community support. Merging the two together wasn't my best idea for an up-sell.

While I'm not very aggressive about this, my greatest success with an "up-sell" has been offering book editing on my website. It's not exactly the most natural step for many of my readers, but with the growth of independent publishing and self-publishing (more about those terms later), it has worked out that many people who want to publish a book can make it happen. Simply having information available about my publishing services is often enough to bring in new clients. I've also ended up with people who contacted me asking if I could fix a computer or install a printer, so my system isn't exactly fine tuned by any means!

I don't want to lead you astray from your personal and ministry goals in writing by talking at length about these up-sells. I especially don't want you to start obsessing about all of the ways you could make more money. Rather, I want to help writers, who feel especially called to write, discern sustainable ways forward for their work or ministry. Don't force an up-sell. Rather, remain open and aware of ways you can naturally expand on the work you've already done. I honestly don't give up-sells a ton of thought, but I would invest a little bit more in them if our family's main source of income depended on my writing rather than being a dual-income household.

As you consider ways to make your writing work sustainable and healthy for your soul, pay attention to the ways you react to various ideas. It may be perfectly natural for you to build an online course that shares your expertise. I know several former teachers who supplement their writing income by teaching online courses, and it's a perfect fit for them. Just because you know about certain writers with dubious credentials scheming to set up various online courses, that doesn't mean you can't find an authentic way forward.

Writing by Faith

Money can become a creative and spiritual obstacle for many writers--causing them to compromise on projects or measure their success in ways that are damaging and distorted. The pressure to earn more money can inject significant anxiety and distractions into our writing work. It can be difficult to focus on each day's work, let alone what needs to happen in the next year, as we see the immediate need for income right now. I've personally seen how the demand to increase my income puts pressure to submit a project before its ready or to spend my evenings worrying about how I'll increase my income for the next month when I should be spending time with my wife and children or spending time in prayer. As difficult as it's been for my writing work to worry about earning enough money, it's been far more damaging to my personal and family life.

At this point in my career, I have a lot more stability with my client base than ever before, but things can dramatically change with an email or two. I still hold my breath when a client emails me, "Do you have time for a phone call?" Despite that uncertainty, which honestly everyone with a job faces at one point or another, I've moved into a place of greater peace by speaking honestly and openly with some trusted friends and family members. I got into writing in the first place because I simply can't stop myself from doing it. It's a calling that I simply can't escape. At a certain point I learned that trusting God with the origin of my calling to write meant also trusting God with the results of my writing each day.

That isn't an easy line to walk most days. When I started out as a freelance writer, I made some big mistakes in plotting out my career. I'm even more concerned about giving an aspiring writing the wrong advice about making a living. I hope that I can at least point out the places where you'll find the greatest conflicts as a writer who maintains a healthy soul and has flourishing relationships.

If you, your family, and your trusted spiritual advisors all sense that you're called to write, then I encourage you to jump into it. However, we sometimes make assumptions about what that calling has to look like. I started out believing that my calling to write was only valid if I had a contract with a commercial publisher. However, after publishing several books commercially, I saw that my calling didn't hinge on that detail. That was something I'd unwittingly tacked on. When I set out to publish books independently, I felt a lot of freedom and peace. It was as if I'd been waiting ten years just to make that leap of faith.

If I'd opted to go independent right from the start, I would have felt like I was short-changing my calling from God to jump into writing. As I made mistakes and hit obstacles in the commercial publishing field, I often wondered why I felt such a strong calling and still struggled so much. Didn't God call me to this sort of work? Did I choose the wrong career? Or was it possible that I needed to go through a fairly typical process for launching just about any business or new venture?

As I reflect back on my career so far, I hope you can see how tricky it can be when writing gets tangled up with earning a living--especially when God is part of the picture. Boundaries, motivations, and goals can become confusing or at least blurred. Of course you want your writing to reach people if it's a ministry, but at what point does greed or pride begin to interfere? If you feel called to write, but you can't earn a living by writing about spiritual topics, do you feel peace about finding more reliable ways to make a living? Perhaps you can even find writing work for businesses that make it possible to write other projects on your off-hours as a ministry.

I don't want to limit anyone to single approach. We all have our own gifts, can hear from God, and can ask trusted people for prayer support and wisdom.

What do you like to write?

What can you write to earn a living?

Where do you sense God leading you?

As you build a career as a writer, take stock of where you're at each year to make sure you and your family are at peace with each other and with God. You may need to take more risks one season, and another season you may need to seek more stability.

If I could caution you against one thing, it would be this: waiting for God to bail you out financially because you personally (that's the key word here) believe a particular approach to writing is the only path forward, even if it doesn't appear to be working. I have watched people ignore the counsel of prayerful Christians in their lives because of a "personal word from God," and they have ruined themselves and their families financially, mentally, and spiritually by staying the course far too long. Always move forward with the help of prayerful counsel. Take risks when you sense direction from God, but don't stay the course into catastrophe by yourself because you believe you can hear God better than anyone else. I'm a firm believer that believers all share the same Spirit of God. So if you are surrounded by prayerful, caring people who are concerned that you're taking too many risks or need to change course, don't ignore the wisdom that could come from them. If you do pursue commercial book publishing in any way, you're going to need all of the prayer you can get.

CHAPTER 4

SAVING YOUR SOUL FROM BOOK PUBLISHING

Why We Buy Books

Writing books commercially or independently has proven at the very least a reliable source of part time income for many authors, while also providing a substantial income for the most successful authors. While book publishing is typically one of several income streams for writers, those who invest in their craft and pay attention to the basics of the business can certainly earn a respectable income if they work at it long enough. Don't expect a sustainable publishing income to come in a year or two since you won't sell very many books until you've built an audience for your work. Writing for that audience is where we need to begin.

Authors will quickly grow frustrated if they focus on

landing a book deal or independently publishing a book without addressing the essentials of finding an audience and writing for them. In fact, failing to pinpoint your audience and the specific way you hope your book will connect with them can do the most damage to your soul. You'll be tempted to impersonate someone else and you'll remain insecure about your writing to the point that no level of popularity will ever be enough. All talk about price aside, a book is an investment of a reader's time and emotions, and you often only have a few moments to convince readers that your book is worth their while.

When it comes to publishing, we may pick up a book because we know the author or the book offers a particularly gripping story or introduction to information we need. In the niche of Christian publishing, we're looking for an author we can relate to or an author who provides information we need about spiritual growth or studying the Bible. Genre fiction such as romance, mystery, science fiction, and thrillers have proven reliable sources of income for many authors because the audience is ready-made and, in some cases, tightly knit. This is also why Christian publishers look for pastors who have a large church: people already know and trust this person and they have a pretty good idea of what they're going to get from that pastor's book.

At the heart of every successful book is a promise to meet the needs of readers. The need could be as simple as a good laugh or it could be as complex as finding healing from damaging experiences. Perhaps this all sounds like common sense, but this foundational premise is where so many new authors struggle. Even experienced authors have to work hard to narrow down what their books offer readers and why they should be trusted to deliver.

In the case of fiction, an enticing, well-written description and some five-star reviews may be just enough to tip readers in your favor. In the case of nonfiction, readers may be swayed by the author's credentials, real-life experience, a trusted endorser, or a combination of reviews and the sample on a retail website.

During a talk at a writing conference, an agent talked about how people browse for books at a store, and he demonstrated this by flipping a book around in his hands, thumbing through some of the pages, and checking out the back cover. That was a bit of a light bulb moment for me. I don't have much of a chance of getting my books into many bookstores, and even if I did, I'm not sure I could convince enough people to travel to those bookstores to find my books in particular. A very small number of authors have books in stores and can successfully drive significant sales through brick and mortar stores. However, we can all send potential readers directly to online retail sites like Amazon, Barnes and Noble, Apple's iBooks store, and other independent or small retailers.

While I already knew how to shop for books on Amazon, checking for reviews, endorsements, price promotions, and samples before making a purchase, I had to immerse myself in the world of eBook readers. In particular, I had to learn this: How do these customers read books, find new books, and make purchases? For instance, Nook users know there's a $2.99 and under list you can access for the latest bargain deals, while Kindle users know how related books are recommended at the end of a book and how to find the free bestsellers and the regular bestseller lists. I use both Nook and Kindle e-readers, and it's pretty uncanny to see how the books on my Nook end up being on the list of reading recommendations on my Kindle.

If you've ever used an e-reader, you probably know that you can highlight text and either save it for later or share it on social media. In the case of Amazon's Kindle, you can even make your highlights public so that they'll show up at the end of the book's sales page. This is a huge selling point for a prospective buyer, especially in the case of nonfiction. In a matter of seconds, a reader can scan through some of your book's best content and decide whether it portends good things to come.

I still love book stores, especially independent bookstores that serve as the cornerstones in many communities, but most authors hoping to make a living need to realize that the typical bookstore will not return their calls about setting up book events, let alone carry their books. In most cases, only the top tier of authors may be able to land a high profile interview on NPR or in a major newspaper that prompts listeners to look for their books--books that are waiting in the front of Barnes and Noble in a face-out position that a publisher paid for. An independent bookstore may maintain displays of Booker and Pulitzer Prize winning books, but that won't apply to the majority of us. I mean, if you CAN manage any of those above things, go for it! However, the rest of us need to think about how we're going to present ourselves and our ideas in largely online retail formats so that potential readers are able to discover our books AND buy them.

I'll review some of the commercial and independent publishing options in this chapter, but your ultimate decision rests on how you hope to reach readers with your ideas or story. Speaking from first hand experience, it's really easy to get so caught up in the book idea and the need for it that you can forget about how readers will find it and whether they'll be motivated to even buy it when they do find it. Who are these readers? Where do they hang out? What are they thinking about? What are their problems? How are they finding books? What will put them over the top in picking your book out of the millions of other books available?

Your answers to those questions will determine which option you choose to publish your book.

Choosing Publishing Options

If you're going into book publishing in order to only make money, you'll most likely be deeply disappointed--at least at first. Writing books may be a source of income, but if publishing is your family's only source of income, you're basing your financial security on doing something that very few people do successfully.

While I am one of the many authors who started out with the life goal of publishing a book commercially, I wish I had muted the romance and drama of that dream to think of things a bit differently. A book is just one of many ways to share ideas or a story. Mind you, books are my favorite way to share ideas and stories, but I became so fixated on commercially publishing a book in order to validate my ideas that I overlooked other ways to reach readers that, ironically, could have helped move my publishing career forward much faster than it did. For instance, I had overlooked the value of sending monthly newsletters with my in-process ideas or hosting discussions on Twitter or Facebook around topics I'd been hoping to write about. The feedback and reactions of readers, friends, and even social media users I didn't know have since proven invaluable in my publishing work while also cluing people in on what to expect from me in the future. I also wish that I had invested more time and energy into writing short eBooks that distill a smaller idea from my longer books and can potentially reach more readers.

Each publishing option has inherent advantages and disadvantages, but it's more important to decontextualize these pros and cons in light of each particular publisher.

The editing and marketing support from publisher to publisher will vary significantly. I will say that while I personally found the experience of commercial publishing extremely educational and helpful in many ways, I also veer toward a preference for independent publishing as of this writing. Most tragically, I've met too many authors who immediately start thinking of landing a commercial deal before looking at the other options available--options which may be better suited for their careers, audiences, and lifestyles.

Most tragically, too many talented would-be authors wait for a publisher to choose them before they consider themselves legitimate authors. I have found that too many talented would-be authors toil on highly successful blogs and bear the disappointment of never being chosen by a publisher or never working on a proposal long enough to even submit it, while "authors" with a handful of connections with readers send off proposals to publishers unaware that their creations will just languish in an assistant's inbox before being scanned briefly and rejected. By all means, do the hard work of identifying an audience, building connections with readers, and practicing your writing, but don't let a publisher determine whether or not you will publish a book. If you've done the work of building some sort of foundation for your publishing career, such as building a successful blog or email list. You don't necessarily need a publisher's permission to write a book for those readers. There certainly is something valuable in the vetting process that many authors go through with a publisher. Nevertheless, any writer committed to the hard work of book publishing, especially the rigorous editorial process, can create valuable books on their own and potentially even reach more people if they read a few books on marketing.

When I hear from aspiring authors trying to sort out

their paths for publishing, many find it quite difficult to weigh the risks and benefits of the many options that are now emerging. For instance, there are large, medium, and small publishers around who still operate with a royalty model offering between 12% to 15% of sales in most cases. The larger the publisher, the more likely the publisher will offer an advance, with the majority of advances providing the rough equivalent of one to three months of salary for the average American worker, depending on your location.

However, the benefits and risks of small publishers varies considerably these days. While its true that some small publishers have done a valiant job in promoting their authors, others are far more risky. For instance, there are many new publishers who have just launched and have little to no experience in successfully marketing the books they publish--the key word there is "successfully" as they will surely offer all kinds of services. These smaller publishers may send flattering emails to would-be authors and offer either publishing packages for a set price or a subsidy set up that requires purchasing a pile of books. The publicity they provide is often inferior, if not downright counterproductive, and in some cases these small publishers simply fold and could leave their authors unable to reclaim the rights to their books. Remember, some of these small publishing houses are set up by people with zero publishing industry experience, so who knows what the contract terms are or whether they'll even bother fulfilling them before moving on to the next scheme.

That is certainly the worst case scenario, but I've seen it happen to my friends. I've also seen promising authors choose a flattering small publisher, that is virtually brand new and unknown, rather than investing in their work for a few more years in order to get noticed by a larger publisher with a better track record or releasing their books independently, covering the editing and design costs, and placing themselves in a position to reap the majority of the financial benefits if things work out. In a best case scenario, a small or medium publisher will provide excellent editing and design before helping their authors identify a particular niche where they can best use their resources. I've seen small publishers throw "surprise release" events where they lined up a bunch of people to promote the book as a kind of surprise party for the authors. Small publishers can also go deeper with particular niche communities and may present excellent opportunities with a specific audience subset.

Too many authors assume they need a publisher, when, in reality, they could potentially manage the process quite well on their own by hiring a few professionals along the way as they release their own books independently. I brought the figures from one of my royalty statements and my independent publishing sales numbers to a meeting with an aspiring author, and it all clicked for him. He saw that he could get his book in front of more people on his own, even if I had really good things to say about the experiences I had with my publisher. I'll add that my friend in this particular example was a bit more entrepreneurial and far more concerned with simply getting his book in front of as many people as possible and not necessarily maximizing his profits. However, it's likely that his generous approach at the outset could better position him to make more money in the future when he releases additional books.

At the outset here, we need to make it clear that every would-be or established author has plenty of options. You can go straight independent, exclusively commercial, or a mix of the two. There are advantages and disadvantages along the way. I know commercial authors who are extremely happy, and I know commercial authors who are extremely disappointed and jaded. I know independent authors who are successful, and I know independent authors who are struggling. You can find anecdotes all across the board. The most important factors aren't whether you can find horror stories or success stories. They're out there for sure if you look for them! The most important factor is which publishing options line up with your calling and make it possible to care for your soul while pursuing your writing career.

For instance, since my entrepreneurial friend realized that his writing is a ministry, he simply wanted to get his book in front of as many people as possible without worrying about making a profit. While he hopes his work will lead to a small income, it's more important to get his book in front of people who will benefit from his message. Once we clarified that goal, we were able to talk frankly about what a publisher would require and offer in light of his options as an independent author. Tools such as NoiseTrade, Kindle Direct Publishing (KDP), Draft 2 Digital, and robust DIY website services such as SquareSpace make it extremely easy to provide eBooks to customers at little or no cost. CreateSpace also makes it possible to offer cheap Print on Demand copies on multiple platforms or to produce author copies to hand out or sell at cost.

Having said all of that, independent authors hoping to make at least a part time income from their books have options other than giving their books away like my friend. The main advantage to creating a book completely on your own is that you have significantly more control over your price promotions and other marketing opportunities. While your reach could be limited compared to authors working with a publisher, you may have other tools available to reach more readers that commercial authors simply can't use. For instance, one of my publishers will not run sales on Amazon for my books. It's just not an option for them. Even on their own site they won't run promotions at the price points that eBook experts recommend. They have certainly spent a lot of time and resources promoting my book in other ways, but my sense all along has been that my book simply won't thrive using those strategies. It can be tough to watch a book fail because you can't promote it in the ways that you think will connect best with potential readers who may not buy my book because they don't know who I am and need an added incentive to try it out.

If you're hoping to make it financially as an independent author, you need to think about how to reach thousands, not hundreds, of potential readers first. Only a small fraction of the people you can reach will actually give your book a shot, so these are big numbers we're talking about here in order to get even a small number of sales. In addition, you most likely need to think of how to write a series of books that are connected with each other to a certain degree. Once again, there are exceptions here. However, most independent authors who make anything close to a part time income from book publishing write series of books that build on each other.

Almost every independent author I know insists that this is a slow build that takes times. Along the way it helps immensely to have experienced guides who can show you what to do and what to avoid. It's one thing to find a book or a blog post with 50 book publishing and marketing ideas, but it's quite another thing to find an expert who can point you to the three or four things that are proven to work for an author such as yourself.

Most importantly, the publishing option you choose will also play an important part in the state of your soul. I have spoken to several authors who landed dream deals with top notch publishers. While I have envied their success at times, I've also seen how much pressure their deals put on them to sell a ton of books during the first month of release. In fact, authors with traditional publishing deals tend to struggle mightily during the months leading up to their book releases. I know that I have been distant from my family and worried about lining up every piece of promotion. This can be true for independent and commercial authors, but only one of those options offers a relief valve where you can determine your own pace. The exception, of course, being those who are independently wealthy and who can hire someone else to market the books for them (not that I recommend that!).

Publicist Tim Grahl has several approaches to marketing books, with one being the "best seller" launch where you aim to sell a ton of books in a few months so that you land on some bestseller lists. His other option is the "long game" approach where authors figure out ways to promote their books each week. The long game can be as intense or relaxed as you like. It could be podcast interviews, blog guest posts, social media promotions, a new post on your own blog, an ad campaign, or a special promotion to your email list or a segment of your email list. While it certainly helps to pick up a bunch of sales during a concentrated time period, a bestseller launch removes significant pressure and allows time for experimenting. You may launch an independent book, muddle through six months of paced publicity and discover that you either can't bear to manage the process on your own or you can't imagine having the pressure of publisher.

We're all wired differently. We all have family and work situations that are uniquely our own. I have personally found that my soul needs space and time to be healthy during my current season of life where we have small children, so I am very cautious about pursuing commercial publishing and reviewing the marketing support the publisher provides. If I do pursue commercial publishing, it's because I want a publisher's help to make a book succeed, not because I need a publisher's validation. In fact, whichever publishing option you choose, your success will depend largely on whether you can find experts who can improve your book and help you put it in front of the right audience.

Finding Expert Help

Literary agents have been a moving target in the publishing world lately. Some agencies are constantly innovating and offering new services such as marketing help and even self-publishing services, while others stick with managing relationships between authors and publishers. Some have a lot of power and influence, while others serve as intermediaries between authors and publishers without necessarily making waves.

In the Christian publishing world, an agent can be especially valuable in helping authors stay on top of the trends at publishers and resolving conflicts that may come up--especially the unique challenges that Christian authors face when it comes to disputes over theology or a publisher's particular stand on a hot button moral issue. Agents know what a publisher will tolerate and what will raise a red flag. In fact, some agents have their own standards, such as the agent I met who will only represent Christian fiction that is free from profanity. I suspect that some authors will find that unthinkable, while others wouldn't dare to drop a profane word into their manuscripts in the first place.

We could say a lot about what agents do. Perhaps they're best known for their work in placing book proposals in front of editors. Many publishers will only review a proposal that comes directly from an agent, although some of the smaller or mid-sized publishers are starting to work directly with authors. However, this critical aspect of their work really is a small part of the time and value that they offer authors. While a professionally written query letter and an established relationship with an editor can only help your book, agents can also save you a ton of time by evaluating the merits of your book proposal, offering feedback, and helping you position the project for success. That service alone is well worth the cut they take from your advance. By the time an agent opens the door for your book at a publisher, your proposal will almost certainly be far better positioned to succeed because they've evaluated your work with a trained, critical eye.

A nonfiction book proposal, in particular, is a truly unique piece of writing because about the first half of it should be high quality copywriting, while the other half should be a well-written sample of your book. The first half should clearly explain the need and focus of your book, demonstrating that you have the ability to authoritatively address that need through a high quality book project. Most authors, who would far prefer to get on with writing the actual book, would rather write terrible first drafts for the rest of their lives than do this kind of writing. A good agent should at least know what works and what doesn't work in a proposal, and they can help polish novice attempts at copywriting.

Besides securing an editor's attention in the first place, agents also help you negotiate the terms of your contract and any disputes down the line. The latter is really important for authors. Just as we can't imagine a tragedy befalling us such as a threat to our health or a natural disaster, most authors can't imagine they'd have contract disputes or conflicts with their publishers some day. It's particularly tricky in the Christian publishing world where everyone is supposedly a "brother or sister" and books are all about "spreading the Gospel" rather than any personal agenda. The reality is that publishing is a high risk profession where the staff at publishers go through regular turn over, publishers shut down, publishers are acquired by other entities, and theological differences cause conflicts.

Not that we should live each day anticipating the worst, but we should approach agents based on these sorts of factors. It's not enough to find an agent who can competently put your book proposal in front of an editor. You need an agent who can provide feedback on your work, advocate for you during contract negotiations, and look out for your best interests if your relationship with your publisher goes south. I've had one book project cancelled after writing the first draft due to changes at the publisher.

In other cases, my books have run into snags where staff at a publisher were unwilling to try out certain promotions or unable to respond to my emails in a timely manner. In each of these situations, I relied on my agent to work as an intermediary who could speak on my behalf without adding additional strain to my relationship with the publisher. One of my friends had a dispute with his publisher over a theological issue in his book, and his agent actually took his publisher's side! When I talked to my agent about working together, we discussed what I believe, and what I may talk about in my books. I gave her an idea of where I was coming from so that we wouldn't have any surprises down the line.

Agents can do a lot more than improve your book project or approach editors on your behalf. They can provide networking opportunities with their other clients, and they can open doors for additional writing opportunities. Sometimes a publisher may have a devotional or theme-centered book that calls for contributors, and your agent may be able to land some additional publishing opportunities for you along the way. Almost every year I pick up work because my agent sends an editor or freelancer my way.

Some authors are only looking for agents who can manage the contract negotiations for them and rely on fellow writers or editors for feedback on their writing. They rarely speak to their agents aside from checking in every now and then to see if anything has changed. There's really no "right" way to work with an agent. Both hands-on and hands-off approaches can still provide the support and connections that you need for a book project.

As you gain clarity about what you'd like an agent to do for you, you should also keep in mind what you don't want in an agent. For instance, I put a premium on working with agents who aren't put off by my blunt honesty about the parts of Christianity that I find troubling. I also value the fact that my agent is extremely professional and has healthy boundaries. I've worked with some people in Christian publishing who treat me, a colleague, like an intimate friend from small group. They started sending really personal prayer requests and detailed accounts of the challenges in their lives. While I was sympathetic to their needs, we didn't have the foundation in our relationship that would have made that kind of sharing appropriate. And if you think I'm being too uncaring in my perspective there, I may know someone who would love for me to forward some long, detailed emails to you.

No agent is perfect, and I've even spoken to friends who have had vastly different experiences with the same agent. It's only natural to expect that an agent could end up giving a bit more attention to the author who sells more books and lands larger advances! In addition, there have been times when the head of a literary agency may take a different view of a particular author from the agent he/she is working with. When you're researching agents, be sure to also look up their agency and whether you feel like you fit the profile of the other authors there. Mind you, that doesn't mean you need to be a clone of the other authors. Rather, you don't want to stick out like a sore thumb. If the bulk of the authors already represented at an agency write fiction or work with extremely conservative publishing houses, an author with more liberal or progressive leanings may want to find another representative.

Agents don't necessarily make or break your career, but they remain an essential part of the commercial publishing process for many and a good agent can make many critical connections. They act as a testing ground for new authors, vetting new authors before passing their work in front of an editor. Most agents have extremely detailed websites with clear submission guidelines. They have these guidelines for a reason, and authors who ignore the guidelines should never expect a response to their queries. Agents are inundated with proposals and extremely basic publishing questions. If you really want to sign on with an agent, read the top blogs written by literary agents to get a sense of what they expect and which mistakes are the most common for new authors.

Before you query an agent, try to establish some kind of relationship ahead of time by reaching out on Twitter, leaving a comment on the agent's blog, or finding a mutual friend who can make an introduction. In fact, many agents will say they aren't taking on new clients, but the majority of them will review a proposal if an existing client sends it their way. Once I've gotten to know a new author for a few years, I may refer that author to my agent if a project strikes me as a good fit, but I'm also extremely careful to make these referrals the exception rather than the rule-- so don't email me asking for an introduction to my agent just because you read my book!

I've said a lot about agents here, but they aren't the only sources of help for authors hoping to make a living from their writing. Most importantly, your fellow authors will provide valuable insight into publishers, general trends, and feedback on your work. Think about it this way, if you're working alongside authors who face all of the same challenges you do, they'll be much faster to sniff out any issues you may have with your ideas or how they could potentially connect with or miss an audience. Fellow authors can provide the support you need, point you toward opportunities, and share what has worked for them.

Besides informal relationships with authors and formal contracted relationships with agents, author coaches provide a middle ground option. This is something I've stumbled into as quite a few people who read my books have contacted me to ask for coaching. For a set monthly fee I answer their questions, help them clarify their goals, and then suggest action steps to reach them. These conversations have provided a valuable reality check for my clients and helped them reach their goals much faster.

This may or may not come as a shock for you, but many of the publishing and book marketing books available repeat expert advice found elsewhere or fail to provide real help because they are too general. In addition, if you attend a writing conference, there's a high probability that you've just paid hundreds of dollars to sit in a room and hear an agent or an editor to tell you things you could read online for free. If you can sit down with an agent or an editor (as well as some fellow authors!), then you'll most likely get your money's worth out of the conference. However, if you just need ideas for your career and you have a couple hundred bucks burning a hole in your pocket, it will be far more cost-effective to do your general research through reputable publishing blogs and a few select books and then figure out your specific way forward by getting expert advice that is specific to you.

Aside from finding expert help to get started in publishing, new authors most often underestimate the importance of the marketing details in their proposals. Selling books is difficult, mysterious, and time-consuming. I've coached many authors on their book proposals and warned them that their marketing sections are too thin for an agent to give them a shot, no matter how brilliant their ideas may be. Before you invest time, energy, and money in your book proposal, you need to know what will set off a red flag for a publisher.

How Publishers Choose Books

Publishers are always looking for something new and fresh that lines up with what they're already doing. Do you see the fine line there? No? Authors should also be creative and original, but not TOO creative and original. These are the fine lines that many authors have to walk, and that line could look very different from one publisher to another. For instance, one friend of mine wrote a very fresh and creative book about journaling through his struggles with addiction. The book was well-written, bold, and innovative, but it took a few tries before he found a publisher.

As much as I make light of publishers and the choices they make, I'm sympathetic with their challenge to carve out a particular niche where all of their books have a family resemblance without being repetitive. I certainly don't want their jobs! Some publishers do a better job of this than others, but if you're familiar enough with a particular publisher, you should get a sense of what kind of book could fit the best with their existing product lines.

When I started out in book publishing, I had dramatically underestimated how much this niche focus mattered. I assumed that every publisher just wanted a great Christian book. However, I heard on more than one occasion that my project didn't fit with their current plans. In addition, on several occasions a publisher pointed to a project in the editorial pipeline that greatly resembled my own.

By this point you should get the sense that there are many, many reasons why a publisher may reject your book project. It could be that your book isn't their cup of tea, your publisher has too many similar cups of tea, or they don't think enough people will want your particular type of tea. The latter is the most common reason why publishers won't take a chance on a proposal. Even when an editor gave another reason for rejecting my proposal, I've suspected that it was actually tied to my potential for selling books.

If you're particularly interested in Christian publishing, a bit of a reality check may help at this point. For starters, Christian publishers function a lot like other publishers who make the bulk of their income from a small number of bestselling titles. In the Christian publishing world, some publishers do particularly well by selling Bible versions or Bibles with study notes. There's also the ubiquitous Amish romance that basically provides an alternative to steamy romance novels and erotica. We shouldn't be surprised that Christian publishing follows sales trends that resemble the rest of the publishing world--even if our bestsellers are a bit more "buttoned up." Genre fiction is a big money-maker across the board, and Amish romance is simply another iteration of that.

Besides Bibles and genre fiction, Christian publishers know they can reliably make money from either pastors with large congregations or bloggers with massive followings. Both represent a certain number of guaranteed sales. If they're going to take a chance on a relatively unknown author, they need a really compelling reason to take any resources away from the tried and true authors and revenue streams. I know that many editors find books that they personally love but can't justify signing because of the economic realities of the publishing world. It doesn't help anyone to try to blame a particular editor or publisher for this current state of affairs, since I know many of the people involved in publishing are sympathetic with authors trying to find their way. Some editors have even remarked that the writers of several beloved spiritual classics couldn't convince a publisher to take on their projects today--a state of affairs that should certainly give us pause.

As long as the top authors keep the lights on, publishers don't necessarily need a new author to succeed. Of course they would like a new author to succeed, but if a first-time author tanks, as most usually do, they will most likely move on to someone else. In fact, I've heard from several sources that a completely new author has a better chance at getting a book deal than an author with a poor sales history.

Let's say you do end up striking gold and sign a nice entry level book deal with a reputable publisher. The contract terms specify that you need to deliver your book's first draft within a year of signing, with the hope that it can be published six months from then. The reality for most authors is that you should have figured out how to promote that book to thousands upon thousands of people a year before signing that book contract. For the sake of dealing with round numbers, if you've been paid a $5,000 advance, a good goal would be at least 4,000 book sales, provided they aren't at highly discounted rates. Every publisher will have different standards, but when you prepare to pitch your book to a publisher, keep that number in mind. Also keep in mind that telling 4,000 people about your book isn't the same thing as finding 4,000 people who will actually buy it. Can you demonstrate in your proposal that you'll be able to sell thousands of books?

Now may be a good time to check in: How is it with your soul right now? Most of us have never sold four thousand copies of anything, let alone a book that we've labored on for years, affixing our hopes, dreams, and best ideas to it. It can feel like you're sunk before you even begin with publishing. This is why it's so vitally important to lay the groundwork of finding your voice, writing for an audience, and developing sustainable (and effective) ways to connect with it. Instead of throwing yourself at the mercy of a publisher or taking a chance that you'll land a book deal before you'll be ready to promote it, commit to the slow build now so that you'll be empowered and prepared for the challenges that will surely come.

Publishers do take chances on new authors. All is not lost if you're starting from scratch and aiming for a book deal some day. Editors may love your idea. You may know lots of influential authors and bloggers who will help sell your book. You may hit on a controversial topic at just the right time to get a lot of media attention. An editor may have found your project at just the right time. There isn't one way to land a book deal with a publisher. Looking back on my commercial projects, I can see that several factors lined up along the way to make signing a book contract all the more likely.

Mind you, if you can't guarantee thousands of sales and no one wants to take a chance on you, that isn't the end of your publishing career. In fact, you're starting in a place where almost every published author has been: rejection. The good news is that you don't have to depend on a publisher to put out a great book or to build an audience. You can publish your books independently right from the start and then hope to attract a publisher's attention once you've had some success and can demonstrate a strong sales history. While independent publishing is an evolving industry, there are a few details every writer should consider before jumping straight into commercial publishing.

Why Publish Independently

I use the term "independent publishing" or "indie publishing" in order to describe authors who publish books seriously and professionally on their own. Indie author Joanna Penn has written at length about this distinction between indie authors and self-published authors--the latter being those who pursue publishing more as a hobby than a professional career. According to Penn, the self-published author usually wants to make a book and put it out there. The indie author works with professionals and strategically promotes books. You could draw comparisons between indie authors and indie musicians. Most independent musicians care just as much about the quality of their work when stacked up against those signed to major labels. The same goes for indie authors.

I tested out independent publishing in 2010, and I didn't have the best experience with it since I was still trying to promote my books using more traditional tactics, such as soliciting magazines for reviews and trying to land articles in top publications. I tried to get the book into local bookstores and set up events. I spoke at conferences and tried to line up a few guest posts on blogs. I had a few sales, but at the end of the day, it was still easier to work with a traditional publisher in order to write and publish the kinds of books I wanted to release.

The more I looked into independent publishing in the following years, the better things started to look. Most notably, there were new programs and online tools available that easily created eBook formats, print book templates, book covers, and email campaigns that could help authors create and sell their books independently. Distribution options have improved, and there are simpler ways to provide your book through a variety of websites and advertising services.

I'm certain that the tools, tactics, and even formats will change a little bit every year, but for now, here is a brief overview of how I approach my own independent publishing projects. This will certainly change over time, and I'm not convinced that I have the "best" way to do all of this. I've been quite content to use a program called Scrivener to compose my books and then compile them into various eBook formats. I then export my Scrivener project into a Word file and then paste each chapter into a print book template from CreateSpace, the print on demand (POD) service that Amazon offers. I choose the widest distribution possible for my print books, and when I upload my book to Kindle Direct Publishing, I don't choose any of the extra options like Kindle Select that would limit my book's distribution. I also cover the rest of the eBook distributors through Draft 2 Digital.

As for outreach to potential readers, I offer several short eBooks for free on NoiseTrade Books in order to collect newsletter subscribers, and I also offer two free eBooks to newsletter subscribers on my website. I use a simple WordPress.com template with my own domain name and pay the extra fee to remove ads from the site. I've been using a mix of MailChimp and Tiny Letter to send out my bi-weekly newsletters, and both offer really simple opt-in pages that make it easy to offer perks like a free eBook and then automatically send it once they've confirmed their subscriptions. I also list several eBooks for $.99 on Amazon and keep some of my eBook shorts free on platforms that will allow it, such as Kobo and iBooks--

both of which I can manage through my Draft 2 Digital dashboard.

While many authors do a lot less and some do a lot more, I've found that it's not all that hard to manage an independent publishing career if you have a few tools that work really well and you can devise a simple strategy for keeping your books in front of as many readers as possible. Mind you, we haven't gotten into the marketing end of things, which we'll discuss in the next chapter, but just from the standpoint of creating professional, high quality books, I now have a simple workflow that can make publishing on my own even more efficient than working with a publisher where, for instance, I have to sometimes pester various people just to get a decent PDF made for my early reviewers.

Before I found Scrivener, I used to struggle mightily to create a decent PDF or Word file that could be converted into an eBook. Amazon has gotten better at converting Word documents, but it's ideal to simply create every format you need while eliminating much of the guesswork that used to add many frustrating hours to my eBook production. In addition, every time I release a new book, I can open up Scrivener, update the back matter in the rest of my books, and upload the new file in a matter of minutes.

Perhaps you've been reading all of this, and you're thinking to yourself: This sounds like a lot of work. I admit that it certainly is on the front end. There's a learning curve to this independent publishing stuff, but honestly, there's an even steeper learning curve when it comes to working with all of the ins and outs of the publishing industry. From where I stand, it sure seems like you'll have just as many challenges along the way working with people at various publishers as you do with a computer program. Even if publishing commercially is a career goal, most successful authors I know have created short eBooks on their own and used them to build their mailing lists or to thank subscribers to their blogs. So the difference between what a traditional/commercial author and an independent author may not be so dramatic once you break down what both have to do in order to be successful.

I'll be honest, I thought that independent authors were obsessed with control when I first started reading their blogs. Isn't there a place for working on a publisher's team? Must an author control every aspect of the process?

While I certainly send my blessing to any author who can find success while working with a traditional publisher and I've worked with some great people at publishers, I can now see where independent authors are coming from. It's not that they don't want to work with a team--it's that they manage the process themselves, choose who gets to be on the team, and jump on opportunities as they come up. If you've ever been waiting on an editor's revisions and watched a project fall behind or missed out on a marketing opportunity because a publicist didn't respond to your emails or didn't want to try it, then you know exactly why more control can be advantageous.

However, all practicalities aside, there certainly is a bit of a dark side to publishing that we often lose in the midst of our dreams to see our names in print and to take a picture of our signatures on an actual contract. Publishing a book in general can hurt, but commercial publishing can be especially painful. When I talked about this with a group of writers who have all published with large, legitimate publishers, this experience of pain and disappointment ran across the board for every single one of them. Everyone had experienced some sort of disappointment along the way. While independent publishing isn't a safe guard from the pain of publishing by any means, there are more opportunities for negative experiences when it comes to commercial publishing.

For instance, I know many authors who have struggled through the process of gathering endorsements, calling in favors on influencers, and piling up enough marketing opportunities for their books. While every independent book will need to do some of this in order to be successful, I know plenty of authors who have felt extremely uncomfortable with the popularity game they felt forced to play in order to meet their sales goals. Once you get an advance for your book, you have a significant amount of pressure to earn that advance back if you want to publish another book commercially.

If you're working on a book independently, you can play as much or as little of the game as you want. You can opt to not gather endorsements or only approach a few people you feel comfortable approaching. You don't have to call in every favor possible. If your book doesn't sell as well as you'd hoped, you can always try new tactics in the coming months and years. Either way, your next project doesn't hinge on how well your current book sells. When I coordinated my first serious independent book release, I remember being shocked at how stress-free it was. Mind you, I worked hard and definitely had book marketing on the brain in the weeks leading up to release. However, the pressure was entirely different. I simply marketed the book in the ways that felt natural and comfortable for me as my schedule permitted.

The opportunity to control the independent publishing process extends to the control you have over your own soul. It's not that you can't slip into a toxic frame of mind while publishing independently. You certainly can. The difference is that you don't have someone specifying how many endorsers you need, how many sales you need to make, and when you need to promote your book. Having said all of that, I know several commercial authors who work very hard to set boundaries with their publishers in order to make the publishing process sustainable. However, in some cases that can be a hard sell when a publisher is trying to hit a two to three week window for book sales.

When I've talked with new authors weighing the merits of independent publishing vs. traditional commercial publishing, one of the tipping points has been this flexibility to make a book more of a ministry than a commercial endeavor. That doesn't mean that profitable or commercial books can't minister. Rather, authors who simply want to distribute their books as widely as possible without the pressure to meet sales goals can use many of the strategies and tactics of independent authors in order to put their work in front of readers.

Most importantly, independent publishing makes it possible for writers to start building their publishing careers today rather than waiting one, two, or more years for an agent and a traditional book deal. You can begin working on book projects right now, read up on book writing and marketing, test out these tips on actual projects, and build a readership. Provided you're pitching fresh ideas to a publisher, independent publishing is rarely a liability for authors if the books are well-written, edited, and have professional covers. There's really no reason to jump into commercial publishing today if you're not ready for it. All of the tools are available to authors right now, and the lessons you learn from independent publishing can be put to good use if you want to cross over into commercial publishing. If anything, independent authors will be empowered and know what a healthy "writing soul" feels like should they look into a formal book deal.

Theology and Publishing

While discussing publishing and the state of one's soul, there's a sub-category for Christian publishing that presents its own opportunities and challenges. It can be uplifting to work with a Christian editor or publicist who fully understands the spiritual challenges that writers face and provides support, flexible deadlines, and connections with people who can help. By the same token, a writer's soul may be crushed by Christian publishing professionals who overlook soul care or focus too much on the bottom line. How we work together, divide, or misunderstand the challenges we face can change very sharply based on which Christian camp you belong to.

I'll be the first to admit that I used to think about the theological standards of certain Christian publishers as a major problem in every case. If a publisher rejected my book because of my theology, I considered them closed minded. I have since changed my perspective on this in most cases. One day I spoke with an editor who helped me see that I'd been thinking about the theological standards of most publishers in the wrong way. The editor shared that he would be open to acquiring books from a wider theological spectrum, but his publisher had largely made in-roads with a certain group of customers from a particular theological camp. If he picked up a book that hammered home doctrines that his publisher's readers found incorrect, they'd fail to sell books, ran the risk of alienating their regular customers, and leave an author largely unread after investing significant time and money into a book project.

It's certainly true that publishers could stand to include a bit more theological diversity at times. For instance, a Christian editor, with pro-military leanings, who bristles at the mere mention of pacifism being a viable option for followers of Jesus is most certainly avoiding a key teaching of Jesus about loving our enemies. Nevertheless, we wouldn't expect a publisher with a history of publishing spiritual classics to take a chance on a speculative end times book or a "journey to heaven and back" account.

Some Christian publishers have wider audiences than others, and there are always particular cases where one could argue for an editor to make an exception. It's not a black and white matter. The conversation I'd had with an editor simply revealed that the question of a publisher's theological convictions is closely tied with the audience that publisher reaches. The editorial team at a publisher may be sympathetic to an author's perspective on an issue, but editors and publicists may be concerned about selling enough copies when it comes time to accept a proposal.

While I never want to overrule anyone's calling or convictions, it's worth noting that some authors should limit the publishers they query based on theology and audience. If a publisher has a long history of publishing books from the perspective of conservative, reformed theology, you shouldn't try to launch a new reformation by proposing that, for instance, John Calvin missed the mark with his theology. The majority of the readers that publisher reaches simply won't touch such a book, and the editors and publicists won't have the connections you need to reach people who will be interested in your views.

Besides the challenge of pitching a publisher who differs theologically, there's always the chance that your theology or your publisher's views could shift over time. I had a book deal with a publisher who didn't necessarily change its beliefs, but I lost my deal when the leadership decided to publish a narrower list of topics that stuck to their core mission more directly. In another case I talked with a publisher about a key difference in theology with their doctrinal statement, and they gave me a waiver on it since it didn't play into my book's content. For all of the times

I've heard of Christian publishers being rigid and prudish, I've personally be pleasantly surprised at the flexibility, graciousness, and professionalism of publishing teams when my own theological differences have come up.

One of my friends, who was quite open about his beliefs, ran into trouble when the staff at his publisher read a controversial post on his blog. While the post had nothing to do with his book and wasn't even close to being heretical, they raised concerns about publishing my friend's book, which even had a release date and appeared in the publisher's catalogue. While my friend had a signed and executed contract and a finished book, the publishing team ruled that they couldn't move forward with the book.

Of course it was devastating for my friend to see his book deal fall apart mere months before release, but at the same time he certainly didn't want a publisher to release his book if they held such grave theological differences! Authors want their publishers to be enthusiastic advocates. As much as it hurt for my friend, it's probably best that this major difference was uncovered before the book was released. The publicity team could very well be less enthusiastic about promoting a book if at least some people at the publisher believed it to be in error.

This is one of the stranger aspects of Christian publishing. For some, theological differences can even trump a legal contract. I've heard of some authors adding clauses to contracts specifying that a publisher cannot terminate a contract based on the content at an author's blog. While it's understandable that a Christian author who, for sake of example, becomes an atheist may not be able to follow through on delivering a book to a Christian publisher, matters get far murkier when it comes to specific theological convictions. Should a publisher cancel a contract if any author changes views on predestination, the details of eternal damnation, or the literal interpretation of certain parts of the Bible? Where does each publisher draw a line? And even if publishers are comfortable with some theological shifts, some publishers are concerned about the doctrinal commitments of Christian retail stores for their more popular books.

The concerns and challenges that authors face in the Christian market aren't necessarily different from those working outside of it. Every publisher has quirks and convictions that will result in drawing fine lines here and there. This is just a matter of knowing which quirks and convictions to look out for and recognizing how they could impact your book. Every year I see a different author work through some kind of theological issue related to a book project. While I'm sure that these problems are the minority of situations, I'm offering up anecdotal stories since I suspect that most authors keep these stories under wraps.

Once you get through the rigors of either securing a book contract or managing the independent publishing process on your own, you will face what many authors find to be the most daunting part of writing a book: selling it. Let's face it: most of us who started writing books got into this line of work because we love the writing process. While it's certainly fun to talk about our books with potential readers or fans of our books, it's a whole other matter to actively seek out readers for our books. The majority of authors are uncomfortable with the thought of publicizing their books. And even if they can rationalize what they have to do in order to find readers, it's still a leap outside of their comfort zones.

I can't guarantee that anything I write will help you feel better about book promotion, make it feel more natural, or lead to epic sales numbers. I do, however, have a few thoughts and suggestions that will help you at least begin taking steps toward a healthier place in your writing and publicity. If you want to make a living as a writer, you need to at least do some publicity, so we may as well figure out the kind of publicity you like to do and how to keep your soul healthy while doing it.

Chapter 5

Healthy Publicity Practices for Authors

Book Marketing Disagreements and Disparity

There's one variable in book marketing that no expert knows: You.

No one can tell you how to be yourself as a writer, blogger, or author. No book on marketing can precisely tell you how to sell your particular book. No one can predict how publicity will impact your soul. No one can predict which marketing strategies and tactics will be most effective for you and your book.

Take a deep breath in.

Hold it a few seconds.

Let it out.

This isn't a science. There are certain practices that may be more effective than others, but no one can guarantee a particular outcome for a specific author and specific book. Book marketing is the land of trial and error, not the land of sure bets.

New authors frequently make the mistake of comparing themselves to or modeling themselves after authors who are quite different from themselves. The promotion strategy that works for an author with a large Twitter following and lots of influential friends won't work for the author who is relatively unknown but isn't afraid to try out advertising at niche websites. One book from a relatively unknown author may galvanize readers who go crazy recommending and reviewing it, while another unknown author may flop because readers didn't find the concept as compelling or at least as immediately sharable within their social circles.

I have heard of authors who are relatively well known and respected in their fields, but they still struggle to meet their book sales goals. Other authors have done well because a book touched on a current controversy that led to a particular sales bump. I know of one author who benefitted from an organization that ordered his book by the box and landed it on the bestseller charts for years to come.

Publishers try to mitigate their risks by finding authors who are relatively well known and can guarantee a certain number of sales. Popular bloggers and pastors with large congregations are particularly appealing to publishers since they can predict a certain number of sales right off the bat. Authors who have neither of these assets may still land a deal because of their writing, the strength of their ideas, or the influential connections who will endorse and promote their work. However, these authors will have a much more difficult time convincing publishers to give them a shot, selling enough copies to earn back an advance, and eventually writing a follow up book.

If you've worked with several book publishers, you may have the uncomfortable knowledge that publishers and publicists aren't necessarily agreed on the best ways to sell books. For instance, books have traditionally been sold to book stores through sales representatives at publishers who send out catalogues to stores and work to convince owners to stock their books. I've sat next to some book store buyers in a cafe while they were listening to the pitches from a publisher's sales representative. The sales representative had a bin full of books, and he pulled them out, one by one, handing them over to the buyers and pitching each concept and story in a matter of minutes. Each book had to grab the book buyer's attention very, very quickly.

Publishers also purchase retail space at larger book store chains so that their latest releases have prime billing and a greater chance of selling. Independent bookstores tend to rely more on the expert recommendations of their staff in order to make sales, thus adding a human factor that publishers can't control.

Whichever way books end up in local bookstores in the traditional marketing landscape, publishers then work to drum up buzz for their titles by landing articles in the local newspaper, lining up radio interviews, encouraging authors to write for magazines, and sending out press releases. Sometimes a book store event helps the more popular authors or the titles that were most likely to connect with readers gain some momentum. If a book ends up on a bestseller list or wins an award, it's likely that more readers will go to bookstores in order to pick up that title.

I assume that most people reading this description of traditional marketing keep thinking about one thing: What about online sales? Amazon has disrupted this model far beyond just chasing some bookstores out of business or forcing publishers to renegotiate payment terms. Amazon has proven to be both a blessing and a curse to authors. On the one hand, it gives every book a chance to be discovered. The titles in the back of the catalogue or that get a passing mention during sales rep meetings now have a chance to be discovered by readers, especially if that book shares any similarities with a popular title. However, that somewhat leveled playing field has also put a lot more pressure on authors to figure out ways to connect with customers as publishers who are familiar with traditional marketing strategies and tactics have moved into digital marketing with mixed enthusiasm.

As tools, services, and personnel change, it's likely that commercial publishers will become more adept at online marketing. However, for now, authors often hear lengthy exhortations at conferences and on blogs about growing a platform or following of readers who will buy their books. This is precisely where many authors, who love to write, begin to struggle. Every publisher has a different emphasis, a different number that defines a critical mass for marketing, and different expectations. Mind you, an author with a large enough following or a good enough idea may become the exception to certain rules. However, the pressure to jump through all of the publicity hoops can lead authors to an unhealthy place as they begin comparing their subscriber numbers, measuring their work by views or shares, and pushing out content to their blogs or the blogs of others that may not be refined enough.

Even if a publisher puts a lot of time and money into a more traditional book launch campaign today, it will most likely fail. It's incredibly tough to sell books through radio interviews unless you're on a nationally broadcast show, and even then, people may find you a fascinating guest but they won't spend a dime on your book. There are always exceptions--big, huge, successful exceptions--but the majority of us need to figure out ways to either partner with publishers or with other professionals to build a viable way to sell our books to readers. The traditional way of selling books works for some authors, but there will always be boxes full of books left unsold since publishers make their money with their bestsellers, not the authors they take a chance on. I spent a year working at a Borders Books store, and one of my routine tasks was to seek out books from a long list, remove them from the shelves, and stick them in boxes in order to send them back to publishers. That is the reality many authors have faced over the years: unsold books, disappointment, and a struggle to move forward with future book projects.

The good news is that authors now have many new options to consider for selling their books. The bad news is that most of us will need to sort all of this out on our own or alongside other authors who are generally in the same boat. If you have misgivings, discomfort, and a bit of resistance to book publicity, you're in good company. If you think that selling your books could be spiritually fraught with danger and could do great harm to your soul, you're absolutely right. However, if you genuinely believe that you have a message to share and you've put in the work to present your writing in a way that could appeal to readers, it's worth asking whether you can find a way to share your work in a way that doesn't detract too much from your writing or bring complete misery.

There are plenty of ways that book marketing can go down in flames, but just because the worst could happen, doesn't mean the worst has to happen. By intentionally talking about healthy publicity practices, trying out some different strategies or tactics, and hanging onto what feels healthy and authentic, we can begin to build a more sustainable writing career that reaches new readers and sustains a reasonable income. While we can talk ourselves to death with platforms and publicity, let's dig a little deeper into why this feels so yucky and can be so challenging for authors. Perhaps calling out what could go wrong will help us see what could go right.

The Tensions of Marketing Platforms for Christian Authors

When I talk to fellow authors, there may be no greater struggle than finding a way to share their books with readers without pulling themselves away from the craft of writing or engaging in practices that feel self-aggrandizing. In addition, Christians authors also know that Jesus said things such as "the meek shall inherit the earth," but a marketing plan reduced to the word "Meekness" may set off alarms with a publisher's publicity team. Independent authors need to figure out their own ways of reaching readers, and the loss of writing time is all but inevitable. The big question, however, is whether a Christian author, whether commercial or independent, can actually promote a book and remain meek.

My friend Matthew Paul Turner used to work in the Christian music industry, and he notes in his memoir *Hear No Evil* that Christian celebrities have a way of pursuing fame without making it look like they're pursuing fame. We may well imagine an author who repeatedly says that the sales numbers or blog subscribers don't really matter, it's all about faithfulness, but then he pours over charts, graphs, and reports every evening to figure out ways to grow his publishing empire. Ironically, whether you're in a healthy place with writing and publicity or you're living a double life like our fictional author here, you may hear both groups using very similar language. The reality is that numbers can matter, faithfulness is more important, but each need to speak within their proper boundaries. Most importantly, we need to reframe how we think about marketing.

In his book *Your First 1,000 Copies*, publicist Tim Grahl writes that marketing is basically the act of making lasting and meaningful connections with readers and being relentlessly helpful. So while numbers don't necessarily matter in the grand scheme of defining our worth, if we are creating something of value for readers, then it stands to reason that we want to find the most effective ways to keep in touch with them. In other words, spend more time thinking about ways you can share your work with a few more people every day rather than worrying about reaching a goal that some other writer has set. If your book is going to help readers, then don't worry if some don't want to read your book. That's fine. It's only there to help after all.

I would add that I've often been in situations where I wanted to subscribe to a blog, follow an author on Twitter, or learn more about a newsletter, but the writer didn't provide those options in an easy to find location on her website. She was so concerned about not appearing pushy, that she didn't offer a simple way for readers to choose to read more of her writing! Authors can also make this mistake through neglect, bad planning, or shoddy book design.

For instance, I spent years collecting blog subscribers at my first website, but when it was time to change my website, there wasn't an easy way to transfer them based on how I'd set it up. While some migrated over to my new website, I couldn't shake the feeling that I'd wasted years of hard work. These days I focus on collecting blog subscribers and newsletter readers through email and manage both through MailChimp, a popular email marketing program. Whether or not you share your work on social media or though email, if people end up at your website and you want to increase the odds of them returning, consider how you can make it easier to get in touch with them.

I used to worry that I didn't have enough subscribers or email addresses, but those worries prevented me from valuing the people I was already writing for or paying attention to the ways new readers could find my work. We'll talk about sustainable and healthy ways to reach out to your readers, but it's far more important to first lay the foundation of making connections with readers. If you don't have a good way to connect with your readers, then your outreach, whether healthy or unhealthy, won't do any good.

You could ask potential readers to follow you on Twitter or Facebook, but social media can be difficult to control and could be subject to the whims of new algorithms. Your Twitter followers may only see a fraction of your posts if they have you on a list they regularly follow, and then again, you could be one of thousands of friends, brands, and authors who just fly by their feed without a notice. Facebook remains a really effective way to connect with readers, but Facebook has notoriously changed how frequently posts from their pages show up. Even your friends may miss the updates that you consider your most important. Even if you do manage to reach a lot of people on social media, prompting these followers and friends to purchase your book is a whole other matter.

You have a very tiny amount of space available to convince them to spend their time and money on your book. We'll come back to social media a little later in this chapter, but I want to frame our discussion around the challenges authors face in making connections with readers. Social media can help, but it's hardly the silver bullet that so many people make it out to be. If anything, social media will help you build connections by other means (such as a newsletter that you promote on social media or your blog posts that are shared on social media), and those other means will help you sell books in a more sustainable way.

The best way that you can make a long lasting connection, at least as of this writing, is through email. Whether you gather blog subscribers over email or you build an email list, this opportunity to directly communicate with potential readers saves you from having to play games on social media and turns book promotions into more of a conversation. You can literally just be yourself in an email. Mind you, what you email should be helpful, unique, and valuable. There are best practices for writing emails (usually keeping them short, to the point, minimizing design bells and whistles, and making paragraphs painfully short). However, there are no best practices that govern how you can be yourself. Best of all, if you want to just write, you can do exactly that in your newsletter or on your blog.

In addition, too many authors worry that their blogs drag them away from the craft of writing a book. While it's true that sometimes the book or the blog needs our full attention, I fully believe that those committed to writing books and improving their craft can use blogs and email newsletters to improve their writing. For starters, you can test out book or chapter ideas in a blog post. The immediate feedback can push you in new directions that may connect better with readers. If there is no response, then you'll know to consider writing something else or changing your perspective. If you have a book drafted, why not include short passages in your newsletter? You can encourage readers to offer feedback and give them an early preview. Presuming that you want people to read your books some day, newsletters and blogs are two simple ways to begin testing out your ideas and building an audience.

Speaking of audiences, the better you know your

audience, the easier it will be to put your work in front of them. If you join or start a Facebook group related to your book topic, if you guest post for bloggers who share your interests, or do round ups of your favorite blog posts from the past week, then you'll naturally find new readers. It's going to take time, with most authors connecting with just a few readers each week. However, if you find someone selling a fast, high pressure way to "explode" your readership, then the tactics will most likely be dubious, if not a bit slimy and ineffective. The good news is that slowly and authentically building your readership means it will be stronger and more committed.

Your readers will be especially committed if you understand where they're coming from and what they want. I think we've all read books that felt like an author has been inside our heads. They speak directly to the kinds of struggles, concerns, and needs that have been at the forefront of our minds. We wouldn't think twice about them promoting their books because they're offering something we need. We may even try to help them with their promotions by recommending their books to friends or sharing their books on social media.

So long as you're focused on ways to help your readers, you'll have a much easier time thinking about marketing. Rather than making a book project all about sales and numbers, focus on specific readers, what their needs are, and how your book will meet them. Then your creative work becomes more of a gift than a commercial endeavor. When you start thinking along those lines, your writing becomes more of a ministry, even if there's a commercial side to it.

While we're thinking of writing as a service or ministry to others, let's step back and think of a church or ministry. Let's say that a pastor or ministry leader begins to alienate people and people stop attending. While that leader could plunge forward, saying that numbers don't matter, the truth is that the numbers could give him/her a clue that something isn't right. Perhaps this leader is failing to listen to others, condemns others during sermons, or isn't relating to where members of the congregation are at. Numbers don't tell the whole story, but they do tell a small portion of it. We could say that if the ministry is a full color, multi-dimensional story, the numbers at least present the two-dimensional, black and white side of things. Numbers don't capture everything and they don't even define the worth of what someone does in ministry, but they can at least capture a small part of the picture that is tough to refute.

Once someone begins to confuse numbers with the whole story and even begins to make comparisons with the numbers of other writers, then numbers have taken on too large a role. Numbers can tip you off that something is wrong and could be done better, but they never tell the whole story. If you just want to write for yourself, that's great. You don't have to worry about numbers. I certainly write specific pieces just for my own personal or spiritual benefit.

I also write certain pieces in order to be read. I have an audience in mind that I want to serve. If no one or very few members of that audience takes an interest in my blog posts, tweets, or promotional emails for my book project, then I have a clue that something is amiss. The moment I turn this lack of interest into a larger commentary about my personal worth or calling as a writer, I've made too much of my sales numbers. No one likes to fail, and numbers certainly don't lie if you're failing to reach a wider audience, but even defining an ideal number of sales, subscribers, or followers is highly relative and can obscure the higher goals of serving your audience.

By the same token, any success I enjoy as a writer will

be fleeting. I'm still learning to enjoy the highs and to remain philosophical about the lows. I have to measure my success according to my ability to write the best possible book and whether that book has helped readers. If readers write notes or reviews sharing how my book helped them, I can count that a success. I still take some time to promote my books because I want new readers to find them, but I don't have a particular number of sales or a specific bestseller list in mind. Most days, my goal is to at least avoid complete obscurity.

You can't avoid losing some writing time in order to market your work. You can't avoid some of the personal struggles that inevitably come up as you face the highs and lows of book marketing. And if you want to make a living as a writer, you need to live with the tensions of developing ways to put your book in front of others without building a kind of self-serving empire. Perhaps the best ways to mitigate that threat is to remain focused on serving your audience and frequently sharing your connections with other writers, especially those who may be overlooked or marginalized in any way.

Finding Readers

At the risk of sounding too simplistic, I am personally convinced that I can give no better advice for book publicity than to find some friends who love the same things and have fun together. I write my books with a relatively small number of friends or family members in mind. I want to pass along books that they'll be excited to read because I'm continuing our conversations and offering something that's helpful. In this sense, my writing is both a kind of ministry and a kind of business. If I'm not actually helping the people I care about, then I may run the risk of simply writing to make money. I hope that most readers can sniff out such books that don't actually aim to help them. By the same token, the amount of time it takes to plan, write, edit, design, and distribute a book properly demands a significant investment of time that calls for a level of professionalism and some sort of compensation. Serving a specific group of readers and earning some income from it places you in a potentially healthy and viable spot.

If you already know where to find the people who will buy and read your book, then you have an important piece of the publishing process already done. Naturally, this means thinking in terms of niche groups and communities. If you're already naturally involved in a community as a contributing member, then it won't take a lot of fancy promotions to get the word out about your book. If people already know who you are, then you don't need to be pushy or beg for help--especially if your book is actually helpful.

Along the way you'll find that some of your close friends aren't particularly interested in your books. That's OK and extremely normal. It will likely be a shock to see who doesn't care and who does. I have some old college friends who read every single newsletter I send out, and meanwhile other friends hardly acknowledge my existence online even though we are in touch regularly. There's no telling who will become an invested reader in your writing.

My dad had a saying in his plumbing business: do what you can, not what you can't. You can't make people care who aren't interested, and if you did try to make them care, you'd most likely just annoy them. So take note of the people who like and share your posts on social media, read your newsletter, or comment on your blog. These are the people who are invested in your work. While you can still put out general announcements, take particular care to thank the readers who go out of their way to interact with your work. These are the people who will most likely subscribe to your blog, read your books, and even share them in their networks if you ask them nicely and personally without pressure, guilt, or pity.

When I started an email newsletter, I was particularly sensitive to any unsubscribes. I saw these losses as a sign that I was either doing something wrong or that I had somehow lost a really valuable asset. At the time I was also trying to present strong platform numbers to publishers who were reviewing my proposals. However, I have since learned that I was looking at things all wrong. You want to focus on communicating with the people who are enthusiastic about your writing. That list of people may be really small right now, but it will grow over time if you keep working at it.

As your list of email subscribers or social media followers grows, you'll lose people along the way for any number of reasons. Some just want the free offer without the follow up emails. Some aren't into your newsletter. Others just want to receive less email. If someone drops off your email list, that's actually a good sign. You don't want to annoy people! You don't want people on your email list who aren't interested in your work. If anything, you want to simply focus on the people who are most interested in your work. Each person who self-selects to opt out is usually indicating that he/she isn't a part of your audience and wouldn't buy your book or read your blog in the first place. Mind you, if there is a mass exodus of subscribers on a regular basis for a sustained period of time, it may be time to review what you're doing. Remember, numbers can tip you off when something is amiss.

If you have a clear idea about which book topics you care about the most, and you're starting to connect with people who could benefit from your writing, the next step is to figure out how to write for them more regularly. Many authors have set up blogs in order to test out ideas and to reach more readers, but you could just as well rely on a series of short eBooks, a podcast, a newsletter, regularly updated (and highly interactive) social media profiles, or more traditional avenues such as writing a newspaper column. The most important thing is that however you write for readers on a regular basis, you need to find a way to get in touch with them on your own terms. This is why email newsletters or email RSS feeds are so popular. Joining or starting Facebook groups can provide a more intimate way to test out ideas, to learn what people in your niche care about, and to find people who can walk with you on your publishing journey. You may even find fellow writers who share similar goals, and you can work together on your various projects.

Once you have a sustainable plan in place that allows you to connect with an audience on a regular basis, the next step is to begin helping each other out. While networking with influential authors, gathering endorsements, and finding new ways to promote your work can be difficult and draining, the process can be a lot more fun and life-giving if you tackle the challenges of promotion with some author friends and some trusted readers who enjoy your work.

Marketing through Networking

We've delayed this part of the chapter long enough. We've talked about how to make marketing and publicity more palatable, healthy, and even effective. We've talked about writing to serve an audience and working with a dedicated group of readers throughout the publishing process. Now it's time to hit the nitty gritty work of getting the word out. We'll begin with some outreach strategies and then we'll end the chapter with some stand alone strategies that work particularly well for eBooks.

If you follow what the supposed experts say, there's quite a bit of mutual back scratching and networking games going on. The game is something like this, you ally yourself with someone who is influential, that person endorses you to other influential people, and if they like your ally and you enough, they'll endorse you. Then you can take the endorsements of these influential people and leverage them to get MORE endorsements from other influential people.

On and on it goes.

Every author should work to build lasting connections with readers and keep in touch with them, but it can be just as effective sometimes to connect with authors or influential individuals who have connections with potential readers and who can help promote your book to them. It's extremely common for authors to do guest posts on blogs, podcast interviews, and articles for high traffic news sites while promoting their books. In each case, there's usually a connection that has been forged with a key person.

It's especially important to reach out to people who share a similar audience not just for the sake of reaching the right readers but because you want to be able to extend the same favor to them in the future as well. I personally never reach out to someone for help unless I think his/her work would appeal to my own community of readers. Having said that, some endorsers are very generous, others are very mercenary. At times it's better to just go without an endorsement or guest post rather than get tangled in a web of asking for favors, returning favors, and measuring which favors measure up.

While these suggestions will change with time and will

vary from person to person, I generally try to make all of my requests for publicity help in a private email or message rather than sending out a public tweet or Facebook post that tags people. I personally feel put on the spot and unable to consider whether my support for a project is actually a good thing for my audience. I also share a few specific suggestions for how my friend or colleague can help. I may suggest a guest post (with one or two ideas in the email), a Facebook post or tweet that I've already composed, or some kind of interview format on a blog or podcast. I make it clear that my colleague can do as much or as little as desired and that "No" is a perfectly fine answer since this may not be the best time or my book my not fit his/her audience as well as I'd thought. I personally think it's important to end my requests with an offer to reciprocate in the future for his/her book projects, blog, newsletter, or podcast. No one wants to be "that guy" who is always asking for favors and never offers anything in return (those guys and gals are out there!).

Publicist Tim Grahl notes that it's still extremely logical to rely on your friends and colleague's social networks for help with promotions. It's much easier to ask friends with hundreds or thousands of followers to help with your book's promotion than to build your own massive following. That isn't to say that you shouldn't develop a plan for reaching more readers. Rather, you'll need a less tribal, limited mentality if you're going to increase your reach. Asking for help and offering to help are both necessary parts of a writing career.

However, things are far more difficult and delicate if you're reaching out to people you don't know personally and who have large followings. These are the people who are literally bombarded with requests for help with book endorsements, guest posts, and, inexplicably, book reviews--as if they have time to read the piles of books and PDF files that are sent to them! I have a few general rules about approaching someone who is influential and most likely has a lot of people asking favors of them.

For starters, I try to match the request to the relationship. If I'm asking for something big, like a book endorsement, I only reach out if we have a common friend who can make an introduction and I'm certain that my book would be of interest if he/she actually had the time to read it. I also try to make my request at least our second interaction so that our first interaction is me offering to help with his/her book release. Keep in mind, I don't see this is a debt that I expect to be repaid. Rather, I'm making it clear that we're colleagues working together and writing for similar audiences. If we want to help many of the same readers, then it isn't a stretch for me to help them before asking for them to help me.

When I email someone in my network with a request for help, I also offer several suggestions for how they can help so that our interaction isn't a waste if a particular request isn't possible. I've personally found that every author has preferences. Some are amazing at crafting really helpful endorsements, while others would much rather offer a slot to write a guest post, and still others would prefer writing up some interview questions for a blog post or podcast. Be flexible, keep it short, and understand that it may not work out this time--or ever.

Whether you're writing an influential author or a blogger friend you know from social media, avoid sounding desperate, frustrated, or in need of pity. I've actually had a few people reach out to me with emails that began something like, "I've reached out to many popular bloggers and authors, but they didn't even respond to me... I hope you'll help." When you're asking for help with a book project, you really, really want people who are going to be enthusiastic and excited. You also don't want them to feel like a last resort! That may limit your options right from the start, but it's far better to begin with a few friends who care deeply about your work than to beg bloggers to take pity on you.

Don't get lost in the urgency of the moment with book publishing. While you'll especially feel pressure to increase your reach with a commercial project where your future hinges on your latest book's sales, keep the long term picture in mind. You don't want to damage relationships for the long term while you're thinking of short term needs. A lot could change over the years, including some chance meet ups with influential authors at writing conferences or events. You could end up joining a group on Facebook and developing a stronger relationship there.

I spent far too many years measuring my own worth and viability based on what other people did for me. I looked at (and still struggle with this) all of the authors who were pulling in big name endorsers and worried how I would ever convince them to help me. You can waste a lot of time, stress, and anxiety over who's who, who you know, and who you aren't. It can be particularly soul-crushing when you realize that, in the eye of most readers, you're a nobody and it's going to be an extreme uphill climb to get your book out into the world.

Perhaps the best place to start is gratitude for what you have, who you know, and what you can accomplish. If you only have a group of ten or fifteen friends who will help with your book launch, then serve them the best that you can. Having prioritized that, determine to keep meeting new people every week through social media, follow some new blogs, attend a writer's conference, or subscribe to a few newsletters. Continue to value the people who enjoy your work, but look beyond your present circumstances and find ways to connect with people who care about the same things.

Marketing a book can be lonely and difficult. There are plenty of ways you can put your book in front of a lot of people. The trouble is that you don't have any guarantees that your work will pay off. You could potentially end up creating a lot of misery for yourself and your family without actually selling a significant number of books. I often suggest that fellow authors should pick the types of promotions they enjoy and find life-giving and focus on them. You can always do more stuff to promote your book, but your spiritual health and your family's happiness are far more important than nailing every publicity target. If you're committed to working with a group of friends and colleagues to write for a specific group of readers who care about the same things you do, marketing and publicity work won't be quite so stressful or draining.

In addition, with the popularity of eBooks that typically account for somewhere close to half of all book sales most years as of this writing, new and middle of the pack authors have a powerful tool they can use to get their books in front of new readers. As I've learned more about the ways I can promote my books, I've found tremendous liberation in the simple ways I can market my eBooks as opposed to more traditional publicity plans that relied on media and interviews. While the details will certainly change over the years, here are a few general guidelines if you want to promote your books sustainably in eBook format.

Publicity with eBooks

There has been quite a bit of controversy in the Christian writing community surrounding the use of a company that can be hired to strategically purchase copies of your book all over the country in various outlets. The guaranteed result of this strategy, according to the company at least, is that your book lands on the bestseller list. While it's an open secret in the publishing industry that top authors and especially business titles (where the authors have deep pockets and big egos) frequently use this strategy that costs a small fortune, it has been hotly debated whether such a practice is deceptive and immoral, especially for Christian authors.

Although I can't fathom doing such a thing myself, I'm going to assume that the vast majority of Christian authors can't afford such services in the first place, let alone use it effectively. This leaves any debates of its merits a moot point. However, authors now have a different tool they can use in order to bring about roughly similar results even if they aren't quite as impressive to outsiders: discounted eBooks.

A discounted eBook strategy allows any author a chance to at least get noticed on Amazon's bestseller lists while remaining completely on the up and up. This strategy doesn't call for sinking hundreds of thousands of dollars into a campaign that results in a warehouse full of your books. In fact, a limited time eBook promotion is popular with both publishers looking to revitalize their backlists and with independent authors hoping to get noticed by new readers.

I personally like eBook promotions because they don't require all of the soul searching and wrestling with my ego that platform building requires. Mind you, you have to pay in cash for that luxury, but it has often been a fair trade in my mind. You'll need to do a lot of research into your options and make educated guesses about which ones best fit you and your books, but eBook promotions and advertising can remove a lot of personal and ethical issues with marketing your books. For me, a discounted eBook promotion offers a win for readers and a win for authors.

Readers who may not pick up your book after reading a

blog post about it--especially if they aren't familiar with you or your work--may purchase it on sale at a discounted price or if it shows up on a bestseller list at a low price. A limited time price promotion also travels well on social media, lending an urgency and high return, low risk opportunity for readers. Besides eliminating the price barrier, the social proof of seeing your book on a bestseller list also makes readers more likely to purchase it, if only because they can now "find" your book in the first place. If you have strong reviews, a well-written book description, and a really great opening sample available, potential buyers will be all the more likely to give your book a shot.

Mind you, the royalties from these promotions are pretty slim. As of this writing, a $.99 promotion for the typical author nets you around $.35 per download. However, throughout the course of these promotions you'll also see an uptick in print sales and hopefully a little more interest in your other books if you've promoted them in your discounted book. If you have encouraged previous buyers to buy all of your books at once, say for a simultaneous price promotion, Amazon may even show your other books on each book's page.

Once the price promotion ends, you'll hopefully still have enough visibility on the bestseller lists to pick up additional sales at your higher price. In addition, if you make links to your email list visible in the beginning and end of your book, in your author profiles on sites like Amazon, and in any promotional posts you run in connection with the price discount, you'll hopefully pick up new readers who will be willing to check out your future books. So a price promotion doesn't just bring in lower royalties. You're making your book more visible, giving potential readers more social proof before making a purchase, and hopefully connecting with future readers. I have worked with publishers who love price promotions and publishers who hate them. Those who hate price promotions usually aren't looking at the potential benefit of getting a book by a relatively unknown author greater visibility and building up a longer term community of readers. If you're an independent author, especially a new one, a price promotion is by far one of the most powerful tools at your disposal, especially since you can quickly jump on promotion opportunities.

In fact, this strategy isn't limited to eBooks. One author sold his print book for a limited time at cost just to get better visibility and more reviews. Another author sold her print book on pre-order at 50% at a specific retailer just to expand her reach in different markets. While eBooks are undeniably attractive because of their higher profit margins and non-existent overhead, don't overlook the fact that print books still sell well in certain cases and for certain readers. Don't assume everyone reads the same way as you. In fact, you should move into book publicity aware that there are many different kinds of customers who will want to read (or listen to) your book in different ways. If you have the capacity to create an audio book, that's simply one other way to connect your book with a different audience segment.

If you are running a discount on your book either to jumpstart pre-sales and early orders or to breath life into your backlist, you won't get too far by promoting the discount to your existing network. While your friends may help by sharing the discount with their social networks and reach some new readers, you'll most likely have to consider both free and paid promotions. For instance, there are several services that operate through Twitter, Facebook, and email that simply need to be notified when your book is on sale. Most of these services will be grateful to know that they didn't have to do the work of outreach to publishers in order to find a book deal.

There are other services that authors have to pay for, but move forward with caution here, as the type of book you've written and the quality of that book (especially its cover and blurb) will determine your next step. In addition, authors are deeply divided over the results and viability attached with paying for promotions. Roughly speaking, you have two options.

For starters, there are the highly targeted advertising services such as BookBub that has email lists focused on specific markets, and you'll pay more or less depending on the size of that list in order to send them free or highly discounted eBooks. Generally speaking, the deeply discounted eBook strategy on a list like this earns the highest profit if you have a list of closely related books that readers will naturally purchase after their free download. However, many publishers use BoobBub discounts to renew interest in titles from their backlist as well. Authors who have professional covers and can clearly meet the needs or expectations of their audiences should do relatively well using BookBub, at least making back what they put into it. I split the cost with my publisher to run a $.99 promotion for my book *A Christian Survival Guide* on the BookBub Christian list, and I hit #120 overall on Amazon and dominated the religion categories at Barnes and Noble for a few weeks. It helped that I had over 20 positive reviews at the time and the book fell within all of their parameters for promotional books. I can't promote all of my books on BookBub since they don't quite fit into a neat category, reach a niche that isn't a good size for a promotion, or aren't quite long enough, but it remains one of the best services as of this writing for authors hoping to reach large, new segments of readers while placing themselves on the bestseller lists for a period of time.

Services like BookBub offer a reasonably good shot at reaching enough readers to make it worthwhile because they're targeted at specific groups and have the critical mass to make a promotion pay off. Once enough BookBub users buy your books, online retailers like Amazon and Barnes & Noble will reflect your higher sales on their bestseller lists, prompting their customers, who aren't on BookBub's or a related company's email list, to purchase your book. Also, once you've run a BookBub promotion, there are many other discount services out there that use email or social media to promote books.

However, there are many other advertising options that authors are deeply divided over. These generally involve paying for an ad on an eReader discount page or for one of many blog posts on these sorts of pages. These are broader, less targeted audiences that may not bring a huge return if your book isn't broad in its appeal and professional in its presentation. The more you know about the sites and who uses them, the better off you'll be. As a general rule, genre fiction authors tend to have the most options, as will authors of memoirs or nonfiction books with a wide appeal.

Lumped into this group are services like ads on Facebook and Amazon. Generally speaking, most authors have been disappointed with the poor returns on these services. I have spoken to some social media experts who have found significant success with a carefully planned Facebook ad, but they have spent significant time studying how pages work on Facebook. I have been largely warned off from using Amazon ads at this point, and I personally find book ads on Amazon annoying. I usually click through directly to a book that I'm interested in buying based on a recommendation or price promotion, so the last thing I want to see is the clutter of a book ad. Trusting that Amazon wants their ads to be successful, that could change as they make changes and test out new strategies.

When I released *Pray, Write, Grow*, I did run a few ads on

Facebook that lead to a respectable number of click-throughs among my page fans. However, I have no way of knowing how many of them converted into sales. Add to the mix that my book was running at a $1.99 discount, and it's hard to know if my sales even covered my expense. However, if you want to just get your book in front of your page's fans for a few bucks, it's not a bad idea to experiment with a Facebook ad, especially if you've had a few days to test out which posts about your book received the most engagement. Once again, running ads for your book is pretty low pressure and not very taxing on your soul. Just try out some different things and see what sticks without getting wrapped up in the results.

While email lists and ads are effective ways to bump your book sales, even with limited time free book offers that increase interest in your other existing books, you have one other soul-friendly way to make book sales: free eBooks. Free eBook shorts have been a tried and true way for authors to expand their email lists and blog subscribers. I have seen many successful commercial authors move in this direction to reach new readers since many of them got into publishing in order to write books, not to become marketing experts. It's extremely appealing to spend your time writing a high value eBook and offering it for free in order to reach more readers. Of course this strategy is a key part of a long term marketing plan rather than a short term book selling tactic.

I have added hundreds of email subscribers every month by offering several eBooks for free through my website or eBook giveaway sites like NoiseTrade Books. I have also made some of my shorter eBooks free on platforms like iBooks through the online book manager service Draft2Digital. While NoiseTrade requires readers to enter their email addresses when downloading a free eBook, my free eBooks on iBooks include very clear invitations at the beginning and end to subscribe to my newsletter in order to receive more free books.

When writing a short eBook to build an email list, focus on something that is high value, practical, and meets the specific needs of your ideal audience. For instance, I basically stumbled into writing a little eBook called *Creating Space* after the birth of my first son. While in a season where I struggled to hold onto my creative calling, I wrote that book to affirm that my creativity wasn't a mistake, it was a gift from God to share with others. This little manifesto has become my single most read work over the years.

I don't think I could have planned out *Creating Space*. We all want to write something that is highly practical and meets the needs of our readers, but I literally just sat down to write in my journal the day after my son's birth and this book started to take shape. *Creating Space* spoke to the deep needs in my own spirit. I was tapping into something that felt urgent and real to me, and as I faced my struggles with candor, I stumbled into a message that thousands of other people have found freeing. *Creating Space* has since brought in thousands of new subscribers to my email newsletter. They're free to unsubscribe after reading it, but a high percentage usually decides to stick around.

Although email lists provide ways to control how you market your books, they are one part of a typical book launch. Perhaps the most challenging part of a book launch is getting your timing right, especially if you're working with a commercial publisher. While every author and book launch will be different, let's look at a few ways that authors can make their launches a bit more sustainable and minimize the chaos or tension they can cause.

Timing Your Publicity

If I'm ever distant from my family and bearing more stress than usual, it's right before a book releases. That pressure and distraction has dissipated some as I've moved toward releasing my books independently. Cutting back on the stress around book releases may be the single greatest reason to opt for independent publishing instead of commercial publishing. Of course, if you're publishing independently, then you also have to spend more time managing the process, developing all of the materials, and making all of the necessary contacts. I've found that releasing a book requires sending lots and lots of emails as I contact as many potential readers or promoters as possible. Depending on how you want to market your book, you could end up sending significantly more or less emails.

Commercial publishers *can* certainly add a lot of muscle and professionalism to your marketing efforts if you're working with a competent and knowledgeable publicity team. If you're not working with responsible, flexible, and organized publicists, then they may become more of a liability at times. However, for all of the added reach that a competent publicity team can add to a book release, the cost to you as an author will be added stress and a smaller window to release your book. You need to make a big splash as fast as possible before the publicity team turns their attention to the next book on their list. Authors typically set up a kind of "launch team" for their books who help with reviews, social media sharing, and other publicity connections. A private Facebook launch group usually works well for this, but some authors have used email as a way to write to their readers and fans.

There is no way to avoid the chaos of this kind of launch. You can only prepare to absorb it better. For instance, resolve that you'll be content with whatever the sales are. Work hard, but don't get hung up on your expectations. Try to get as much planning in place ahead of time. Even set aside significant amounts of time six to nine months ahead of time so you can write up ideas, put materials and graphics together, and build resources such as website pages that provide information for reviewers and launch team members. Take time off from work during your launch if you can and find ways to minimize the impact that the release could have on your family by planning simple meals, prioritizing some time for personal reflection, and processing the tough parts of each day with a trusted friend or colleague.

I've worked with launch teams as both a participant and as an author launching a book. Both can be positive experiences, but I didn't love it. I'll be honest, I'm far more interested in a "Lunch Team." Wouldn't that be great? We could find little out of the way enclaves that have awesome ethnic food or legit New York style pizza, meet up for lunch, and leave things at that.

While independent authors can go this same route and hinge everything on the first few release weeks, concentrating their time and energy on a limited time launch, you can space out your release work over a year or even longer. Just think of a new way to promote your book every week and leave things at that. You can do as much or as little as you want, and that removes a lot of the pressure and stress. Promotion simply becomes a small thing you add to your schedule each week rather than an all-consuming monster that threatens to take over your life for several months. Mind you, this may not be as effective as the industry standards for publicity, but there's no guarantee that either will work any way. Why not opt for the path that leaves you with a potentially healthier outcome?

I'll add this one caveat. I have personally found it

helpful to still use eBook pre-orders and promotions before and immediately after a book launches. There's a lot of value in getting noticed in places like Amazon's "Hot New Releases" tab and getting good traction from pre-orders so that your book gets a good bump in the sales charts when it releases. You don't have to obsess over that if you don't want to, but if there's anything that could help your book get on the map, a promotional price at the very beginning will jump start your sales when you need them the most.

CHAPTER 6

THE COMPARISON TRAP

Why We Need Comparisons

Every new writer constructs a picture of success based on what they've seen in those who have gone before them. This is inevitable, but it can also prove counterproductive, if not completely derailing for your writing career. I've made some good comparisons and some bad comparisons over time, but there's really no escaping the need to compare yourself with other writers. We all need some goals and boundaries to help us normalize our experience. We look at a favorite writer or a friend who is a little further down the path to get a sense of how many social media followers we should aim for, how many email subscribers we should collect, and how many books we should sell. When I coach authors, I basically help them begin by processing which comparisons they should make and which they shouldn't.

We're all approximating what is normal since there isn't a clear goal for every writer. Whether you want to build a huge blog following so that you can make a living through advertising or you want to make a respectable side income by selling books, you'll begin with some basic comparisons of similar bloggers or authors. You'll find out what their websites look like, how they reach readers, and how they keep in touch with fans. It can be an extremely healthy and productive practice to learn what you want to do by studying what other professionals do, provided you don't copy and paste their approaches and goals into your own life.

It will also help immensely if you learn from people who really are similar to yourself. For a season I listened to people who, while similar in outlook to myself, wrote very different sorts of things. The ways they found new readers and kept in touch were very different from my own. It took years to figure out that I'd been comparing myself with people who built their audiences and managed their careers in ways that were quite different that what I hoped to achieve for myself. Once I found people who shared both my outlook and writing style, I was able to consider different paths forward that were both more natural and more successful.

I think many writers get caught up in two extremes when it comes to making comparisons. On the one hand, some lose their sense of calling and direction by making unhealthy comparisons with other writers who are more successful or appear to have what they want. They try to reproduce the exact results of others. On the other hand, writers who try to move ahead without making comparisons of any sort for fear of struggling with the aimlessness, envy, and resentment could hit a roadblock when they run out of ideas for their work. They don't have a clear sense of how to move themselves forward since they've only seen the downside of comparisons.

As we look at measurements for success and the challenges to soul care for writers in this chapter, I hope to show how comparisons can become unhealthy and destructive and to then set up some boundaries for making healthy comparisons that will help us take steps forward.

There's Always Someone More Successful

I'm regularly shocked to hear that writers who are vastly more successful than myself struggle with comparisons to writers more successful than they are. In fact, I've spoken to several writers who, in my estimation, are clearly reaching way more readers than I ever could, but they can't shake the feeling that it's all about to fall apart at any moment. Of course plenty of writers have noted my success in publishing, and I've quickly countered that misguided estimation of my career. I mean, how could I be possibly be "successful"? I have a long line of authors I can point out who are doing way better, right?

I've had to come to terms with the fact that you literally can never be successful enough. When I was just starting out as an author, I read an article in *Writer's Digest* about the ways even a six-figure advance can fizzle out far faster than most authors would like to admit. Even many of the people who are "living the dream" have to claw and scrape to earn a full time living year after year. And of course those with six figure advances are looking at the authors who get larger six figure advances! I've commercially published several books, been reviewed in the top publications in my field, and managed to at least sell enough copies that the majority of my books lasted in print longer than the average book. However, I'm always looking at the authors who have landed larger advances, sold more copies, or gained more visibility because of their books.

While I've lived the dream of publishing a book, that dream was quickly replaced by new "dreams." My original measure of success quickly gave way to new measures deemed a better representation of reality. It's almost as if I can't let myself achieve something. I need to make myself feel bad about what I'm not doing, so I keep setting the bar a bit further out of reach until I'm properly miserable.

In addition, each goal that I've reached eventually gave way to discontent if I was relying on accomplishments for my sense of identity and fulfillment in life. That sounds like the most cliché of all writing clichés, but the drift toward finding your fulfillment a particular accomplishment is difficult to detect. In my case, I started out just trying to earn enough money to supplement my wife's salary, but over time I started to set goals and to envision a particular kind of success for myself as a writer. I began comparing myself to others, seeking accolades that I thought I deserved, and made way too much out of what happened or didn't happen with my writing.

I didn't necessarily start ignoring my family by avoiding them for long stretches. Rather, it was a far more subtle discontent and anxiety that began creeping into my family time. I started spending a little longer on my work before coming home for dinner, I felt the nagging need to check my website or social media accounts when I should have been fully present at home, and the anxiety of keeping my career moving forward stole the joy I should have experienced with my wife and children. While there certainly are some writers with extreme career/family imbalances, most of us are struggling with a less perceptible drift toward our work and away from our family as we try to match someone else's success.

Even when I enjoyed a little bit of success, I've learned that I shouldn't count on it lasting long, much less offering long term fulfillment or joy. Success always fades. Soon enough there's another young, flashy writer capturing the spotlight and receiving all of the accolades. Interestingly enough, I've had many frank conversations with the writers I had envied and I've learned that, more often than not, things were a chaotic, insecure mess behind the scenes and many of them didn't come close to the goals they had set. They struggled to find the next step in their careers just like I did. The markers of success that I'd set for myself suddenly lost their shine once I heard about the struggles of other writers who had seemingly surpassed me.

"Success" isn't always the measure of the best writer. I've watched some authors write books that all of my colleagues agree are mediocre at best, but they sell thousands of copies because they network like crazy and build their mailing lists by leveraging their connections with the most successful authors in their fields. Every author plays this game to a certain extent. Other books break new ground or provide a needed perspective, but it never catches on.

Marketing through networking and connections with fellow writers can truly become a beneficial two-way street between writing colleagues that serves the authors and their readers quite well if there is some natural audience overlap. I'm regularly delighted to hear how people I know have started following some of my favorite writing colleagues based on a recommendation I made. However, some authors spend so much time on the marketing and publicity that their books suffer or they fail to invest enough time in their craft. At a certain point, writers have to come to terms with how much they want to market their work and focus on publicity. This isn't necessarily a false dichotomy. Some can do both really well and then make pots of money.

The majority of writers I know think of themselves as creatives, story tellers, reporters, or artists before they think of themselves as promoters or publicists. They don't necessarily cast aspersions on publicists per se. Rather, they view the writing work as their mission and the publicity work as a chance to build community around their work-- even if the act of doing that feels like a necessary evil some days. Every writer can develop a balance here and discover ways to enjoyably put their work in front of new readers and make long-lasting connections with them in ways that bring fulfillment. Some writers are less inclined to do so. Others haven't figured out the best way to do this yet.

Publicity aside, certain topics are more marketable to a wider group of readers. If you want people to throw journals and fountain pens at you, go to a literature conference and suggest that these authors could learn a thing or two from the genre fiction authors who crank out a new book every six months. Generally speaking, with some notable exceptions, genre fiction such as romance, mystery, suspense, and science fiction dramatically outsell literary fiction. You'll find some of the best literary fiction writers teaching at universities because it's tough to make a living while trying to win a Pulitzer Prize for literature. That isn't to say that some genre writers aren't incredibly talented or that literary writers can't make a big splash financially. Rather, these are the general market trends that the majority of writers can expect to face. Amish vampire romance mysteries set in a dystopian steam punk world will usually win against a masterfully crafted story about the downfall of a once wealthy family that provides a brooding critique of modern consumer society.

Of course, you will also get pelted with notebooks, pens, and wands if you go to a genre fiction conference and suggest that they all need a Master of Fine Arts in creative writing in order to make it as an author. Many of these writers spend a great deal of time learning their craft. Rather, their goals are quite different from an author who is hoping to write a tour de force that alters the literary landscape. Some of the genre fiction available has strong characters and great story lines. Some of it reads like a horny high school student's study hall free write that is 50,000 words too long.

We can't control what people buy. We can't make people appreciate the literary quality of our books, even if we've written the quintessential page turner. I can relate to writers who feel like their books offering substantial and helpful ideas are passed over in favor of books with questionable writing and slick marketing. The worst thing you can do for yourself personally and for your career is to give in to envy. We can't help making comparisons with other writers. That's one of the hazards of the career. You'll always want to know what other writers are doing. However, we can stop ourselves from envying other writers and letting it sidetrack our own work, goals, and personal identity.

How Envy Destroys Us

A potentially healthy approach to comparison begins by looking at the gifts, accomplishments, and practices of others in order to get a sense of what we should do. For instance, I'm always aware of what other authors and publicists are up to so that I can try out my own experiments based on what I've learned. I want to know what worked and what didn't work for them. However, we can fall into the trap of envy when we stop learning from someone else's success and start resenting them for their accomplishments. Envy prompts us to start attacking the accomplishments of others while elevating our own talents or achievements.

We may have some really good reasons for believing we have more talent than someone else who has enjoyed more success. Remember, the authors who win the Booker Prize or Pulitzer Prize typically sell far fewer books than genre fiction authors. However, belief in one's superior talent can lead to envy and a scarcity mindset where someone else's success has somehow prevented readers from finding your books. The generosity of fellow authors who helped me get started has proven time and time again that there are more than enough readers out there, and the majority of the time everyone wins when authors help each other out. We can spend so much time looking at someone else's success that we fail to think about our own work and how to serve our respective audiences. You won't create a sustainable career by envying or resenting the success of other writers.

While every writer should learn from others and should be personally confident in his/her own abilities, once we give in to the scarcity mentality, we distract ourselves, discourage ourselves from doing our best work, and make our success about what others are did yesterday than what we can do today. There are plenty of opportunities for all of us to grow and succeed. I confess that I've had my moments when I've grow frustrated with the success of certain authors, especially when I think they're sharing dubious if not patently false information with their readers. When I see people relying on a pseudo-expert for major life decisions, I want to post everywhere: "Stop reading this stuff!" Of course part of my response is that I have convinced myself that I obviously know better than the pseudo-expert.

I know envy first hand, but I've also seen that it doesn't have to be allowed to spread unchecked. The best cure I've found for envy is to focus on my own gifts, calling, and readers. In fact, it's quite an insult to my readers if I spend all of my time envying someone else's success. I'm essentially telling readers that they're following the wrong writer! When I focus on serving my own readers and give up on the soul-sucking envy that is fed by unhealthy comparison, I can direct my energy toward my own calling and audience.

In a sense, writing resembles the best aspects of Christian discipleship. We don't grow as followers of Jesus by *trying* to live better. We grow as followers of Jesus by focusing on him. When we get our focus oriented in the right direction, our personal conduct will take care of itself. That's why Paul wrote so much about not being "under the law." When you're under the guidance or "law" of the Spirit, your life is changed. By the same token, stop trying to avoid envy. Just embrace your work and let yourself become swept up in your personal calling. Any struggles with envy will be countered once you get a clear direction for your own writing work.

Success as Faithfulness

I once asked an editor at a major publishing company what she recommends for online publicity (such as social media), and she replied, "Work on it until you drop." All of that to say, you can always do more to promote your writing. You can always make a new social media connection or find a new place to submit your writing. Even if you did try to spend the majority of your work time on writing with minimal publicity, does anyone actually want to work on anything, much less social media, to the point of total exhaustion?

Sustainably writing for the long haul means we need to establish clear boundaries between our work and our personal lives through set routines and schedules. We want to have healthy souls and happy families first. When you have the added pressure of providing for your family through your writing, this work/life balance can go spinning out of control.

And you'll always be tempted to do one more thing because you can always find someone else who is a little more successful or whose career seems a lot more promising from the outset compared to your own. I used to think that I just needed to land one more book deal or make one more connection before things turned around for me. I don't really know what my goal was exactly, beyond making a living from my writing. As I moved from one type of writing project to another, I kept stressing out over not being successful enough or earning enough money. While there's always something you can change about your writing work and you may really need to change some things. Take a moment to prayerfully consider your goals, both long and short term, for your writing work. Don't just have a nebulous idea out there like, "To earn a living as a writer." A vague question like that didn't help me, at least.

As I prayed about my writing work and shared the direction I sensed from God, I regularly talked to a few trusted friends and my wife to make sure I stayed on track. I asked for prayer at church and gave things some time to take shape in my mind. I also share in my book *Pray, Write, Grow* about some practices I adopted such as the Examen and praying the Hours that added some needed self-reflection and structure to my days. Along the way, I saw all of the ways my drive to reach some vague sense of success was driving me into the ground. I needed time to chat with my wife, play with my kids, work in the garden, and a read a few books without the nagging sense of my writing career going down in flames. Maybe my notion of success or progress was simply a matter of setting expectations for myself and managing them?

After a lot of prayer and conversation, I finally started to think about my writing work in terms of earning a baseline salary to live on and some modest goals like, publish a book a year and continue to build connections with readers. I stopped stressing over doing all of the things I saw every other writer doing. I just focused on finding enough work to keep us financially stable and slowly building my publishing plan. When I finally focused on those two things, I found it much easier to stop comparing myself to everyone else and working myself to death after hours. Keeping my life balanced isn't easy, but I now at least have better tools for recognizing the moments when I'm shifting too much attention to my writing.

Adding to our sense of perspective here is the fact that "success" is often overrated. I know several successful writers and bloggers who have come to resent some of the attention that has followed their popularity. Once you're recognized as a thought leader on a topic, you may get targeted for criticism. If you respond too sharply, you could be perceived as a bully. However, if you don't respond at all, you may appear dismissive. It's easy to make a false move. Even if you apologize or delete a comment or tweet, someone could have easily taken a screen shot and then a group of people could hold it against you for as long as they like. To make matters all the more complicated, it's hard to catch someone's tone when commenting online. Misunderstandings can quickly pile up, and suddenly the attention you've received for your work could backfire.

Such a scenario isn't necessarily the norm for most writers. I've seen many popular writers targeted for all kinds of criticism, but only a few have experienced full blown controversies. If you're mindful of always being respectful in your comments and replies, no matter how good you think a sarcastic jab may feel, you'll most likely diffuse the majority of the conflicts that could come your way.

It may help to know that success as a writer isn't all it's cracked up to be, but that's no substitute for the peace and security that comes from knowing your particular gifts and calling. For instance, I learned a few years ago that I shouldn't be the leader of anything. Every time I've been placed in a leadership position, I struggled to keep the big picture in focus and worried about motivating others. I'm a detail-oriented self-starter, so while that makes me a valuable team member or assistant, leadership itself mystifies me. There's a lot of freedom in recognizing my gifts and the ways my gifts become a detriment when placed in the wrong position. Recognizing the types of writing, the topics, or formats you are called to pursue can provide freeing boundaries around your life. A limited focus will help you develop your particular talents and serve your specific readers rather than losing time comparing yourself to someone with different gifts and a different calling.

My success as a writer hinges on whether I've faithfully served my readers with my God-given talents. Church leaders talk a lot about measuring our ministry effectiveness by faithfulness and not numbers. The same goes for our work as writers. We have our places to work and serve, and we'll either be fulfilled or miserable depending on whether we accept where we're at. I won't go so far as saying that you need to accept where God has placed you because it's possible that God is calling you to someplace else right now!

Instead, we have the rather obvious and basic task of accepting that we can only move forward from where we're at instead of wishing we were further along or had made different choices. In addition, we can only go so far as our gifts and personal callings. The good news is that we can often do more and go further than we expect. The bad news is that we often focus on the wrong things and the wrong direction. We see someone else's accomplishments and begin to desire them for ourselves. Another person's calling may be the worst thing for us since we may not have the capacity to handle what others have. That is a humbling and freeing lesson!

I finally learned this when a relatively successful author, who had frequently advised me in my own work, landed a "dream job" writing for an online publication that also helped grow his marketing platform. When I saw what he wrote for this publication, I finally asked myself, "Would I ever want to write for a publication like this?" "Would I want to research and write these kinds of articles?" The nervous knot in my stomach was my first clue that I most likely have a different focus on my writing work compared to my colleague. I started asking questions like: Do I want to write blog posts like this person? No, I don't. Do I want to use social media like this person? No, I really, really don't. He provided excellent advice on writing a book, raising kids while writing, and managing relationships with publishers and fellow authors, but I had no desire to imitate his platform or online interactions. There was nothing wrong with anything he did. I reached my conclusion without judgment. I simply didn't have the talent, personality, or calling to follow in his precise tracks.

That notion may be difficult to swallow at first, but the alternative often becomes an endless comparison of ourselves with others that leaves us discontent, insecure, and directionless. We each have to figure out our own paths, even if we can learn a lot from those who have been more successful in different capacities and callings. As I've let go of my hopes to duplicate the success of others, I've found a greater sense of peace with who I am and what I'm called to do. That has made me a calmer, gentler, kinder person. I don't resent writers who have been more successful, and when the successful complain about the challenges they face, I'm at least aware of when I start to resent them!

Each day is a balancing act where we try to move forward one task at a time. If you feel called to write about a particular issue or cause, keep chipping away at it each day, even if you have to spend the majority of your time freelancing to make ends meet. At the risk of pandering, there really is no one else in the world who sees the needs you see. No one sees people from your perspective. God can use that to bless others. However, we'll only see that kind of calling with clarity if we stop wishing we had what belongs to someone else and commit to do the work. If you're committed to your calling to write, you're going to need some clear boundaries around some specific parts of your life in order to make it sustainable for your soul over the long term.

CHAPTER 7

MAINTAINING A SUSTAINABLE WRITING LIFE

Creative Time

If you want to write sustainably and with a certain measure of financial success, you need to figure out a way to block out writing time when you're most productive and creative. For instance, many writers thrive in the early morning since there are minimal distractions and the day hasn't started yet. In addition, it can be extremely beneficial to begin the day with a productive outburst. I've found that writing in the morning, even if it's only writing 500 words, can change my outlook for the rest of the day.

Some studies have pinpointed the 8 am to 10 am time block as the most important part of the day for creative work. Many writers focus on writing during their creative time in the mornings, with some even calling it a day after two or three hours of highly focused writing. While every writer is different, I've personally found that I usually hit a wall around 3,000 words in a day. Some of my friends have talked about "running out of words." When I've tried to work longer hours in order to keep up with two book projects simultaneously, I frequently found diminishing returns. I wasn't just out of words, I was also using up my time for maintenance and restoration.

While I generally do find that I find it much easier to write in the morning, there's another aspect to consider here. If you are able to write in the morning, set a schedule and make it a habit that you follow every day. You need to know that when you begin writing at a certain time of day, possibly even in the same space, you're going to only write. It may be hard to establish the habit at first, but once you get used to a certain creative output each day at a set time, you'll find that it will become much easier to stick with it, even when you don't feel like it. Most importantly, you'll miss it if you ever skip it.

When I worked a day job, I was able to manage my blog, write a book, and write for several publications by writing for an hour every morning, writing during my lunch break, and dedicating one morning each week to writing work. I didn't have kids then, but the principles I established back then have remained the same as I juggle my role as a parent who stays home with the kids for half of the day.

The work needs to become its own reward, and if you can focus on writing during the most hospitable part of your day for creativity, you'll find it much easier to hit word count goals and knock out projects. With good boundaries and habits, you can get more done than you would imagine. In addition, you won't notice this change on a day to day basis, but over time you'll improve as a writer, speeding up your output and writing better material. At a certain point you'll have a better idea of what works and what doesn't work, speeding up both your creative and editorial processes. A few hours in the morning may be all you need to keep on pace for a book project or a client's website.

Of course sustainably writing for a living without crushing your soul also means that you need to think about ways to reach new clients or readers. If you can guard your best creative time for the serious work of writing, figure out pockets of time where you can expand your network and build your audience.

Promotion Time

"I have never seen an author work as hard as you," my publicist emailed after a book release. It was the kind of message that I both wanted to frame and destroy. I consider myself a writer first, and publicity is one of those necessary evils that I engage in. Mind you, I love talking about my books with readers, but the process of always finding new people to read my books can wear me out because it requires calling in favors, pitching articles that may never see the light of day, and always emailing one person after another. It's impossible to ever feel like you've done enough to promote a book.

As tough as it can be to promote a book, all is not lost. The place to begin is in your schedule. While we don't all have the luxury of choosing when we will write due to family or work schedules, my general rule is to try to write as much as possible in the morning and to save any promotional work for the afternoon or, in the midst of a book release, the evening. It's much easier to make a spreadsheet, send emails, or design an email newsletter in the dead time of the afternoon than to work on a demanding creative project. Mind you, there are many days lately where I have to do my creative work in the afternoon and just suck it up due to my schedule. We can't always set our schedules according to the latest research studies. However, if you have a full morning to write, don't let book promotion activities creep into your creative time. Always save promotion work for the times when you need something straightforward to work on.

The schedule you set and the balance of writing and promotion you settle on depends on what is most sustainable for you personally.

Some of my friends feel like blogging takes away from their book work, so they've migrated to email newsletters, speaking events, or podcasting. One author I know even claims that podcasts have actually been far more effective than her popular blog. I personally love to write, so all of my promotion work is tied to writing more. I focus on my blog, newsletter, and books the most. If I ever add anything to that mix, it's often directly based on my writing work, not a deviation from it. If you like to mix it up on social media and enjoy having conversations about the news, then you could focus more exclusively on Twitter or Facebook. If you're more invested in design or photography, then perhaps Pinterest and Instagram linked with Facebook and Twitter are better for you.

A typical month for me involves writing one or two blog posts each week, planning and writing at least two newsletters, and chipping away at a larger book project each day for at least an hour each day (with Sundays completely off). I have ongoing efforts to reach readers such as low price eBooks, giveaways on NoiseTrade, and occasional guest posts for friends or colleagues. However, everything I do aims to reach new readers with my newsletter. I could do plenty of other things to reach readers, but so far this plan feels sustainable while enabling me to keep writing.

The light bulb moment for me with book publicity was the simple realization that I couldn't do everything well. I needed to focus on doing just a few things well. So my priorities are to simply write really good blog posts and newsletters that will introduce my readers to my books. I often take several weeks to work on my posts and newsletters, and I follow a few industry blogs in order to keep up on the latest blogging trends. For my friends who focus on public speaking, they've taken acting classes and other training courses in order to improve their delivery during events. Others focus on creating sharable designs and images for Pinterest, Instagram, and Facebook and have sought out additional design training or expert programs. Once you know what you want to do to promote your book, take some time to improve your abilities. There are LOTS of people doing an average job out there. We don't need more average books and average promotions. We need brilliant books and promotions that will turn heads.

Maintenance Time

There are all sorts of "clutter busting" tips and radical simplicity websites out there about how to sort or remove the junk that accumulates in your home. While I wonder if some of these people with sparkling clean websites about removing clutter write from homes piled high with junk, I confess that I am drawn to minimalism and simplicity. I've noticed that clutter can lead to a spike in anxiety and a lack of focus. If I'm disorganized in work or my personal schedule, I struggle to focus. Suspicious as I am of some minimalist websites, I love their focus on the concept of personal maintenance. Maintenance doesn't need to be a major part of your schedule, but if you don't have it, you'll begin to struggle to keep up with the many little things that fall through the cracks.

For starters, at the end of every work week, I plan out the stuff I need to do next week on a post it note. I list the "must do" projects at the top of my list for each day and then the rest of my ongoing projects in order of priority. While I'm personally most invested in my writing work, I often make freelancing projects my top priority each day since my publishing income, at this point at least, remains feast or famine around my book releases. In addition, I include a few ongoing projects on my weekly "to-do" lists to make sure I'm keeping on track. For a bigger project like a book release, I'll sometimes hop on a more robust organization program like Trello to track all of the small tasks that can pile up. I personally find that I need to spend a little time organizing my daily goals, but if the system demands too much time or too steep a learning curve, it becomes counter productive. I'll just drop it and feel guilty for not being an amazingly organized person.

If I don't clear off my desk and organize my schedule, my mind can easily wander. There's always something else to do around the house. There's always a minor, unimportant task that's easy to do and can replace my higher priorities. Sorting out bills and clutter on my desk weekly ensures I'm freed up to focus on what's most important on Monday morning when I sit down to work on the first task on my list.

Sometimes I believe the lie that everyone else is disciplined and focused naturally. I've told myself that I'm just a terrible person who lacks the ability to focus on my work. The truth is that we all start out with habits and practices that are weak and in need of being strengthened. Each time you work on a new habit, you're creating strength that you can continue to build up over time.

Habits are a bit like breaking trail for cross country skiing. At first, you have to break through the fresh snow piled up on the trail and it's exhausting. You won't be able to ski too far, and you'll second guess your decision to go out skiing in the first place. However, the return trip on your broken out trail will be a bit easier. If you return to your trail the following day, you'll find the going a lot easier, and you may even venture a bit further, break new trail, and continue to expand the distance you can ski each day. Besides the progress you're making on the trail with your habit of skiing each day, you're also building up your own strength. You may even grow to enjoy how you feel while skiing or at least after your work out. If you've ever developed an exercise routine, you know first hand that the work out itself eventually becomes its own reward. The same can hold true with meeting writing goals each day.

The simple habit of making a weekly schedule ensures I know exactly where to start each day. I use social media as a work break once I've accomplished a major task, and seeing a list that is mostly crossed off has been an excellent point of satisfaction at the end of the day. In the writing profession, it can be tricky to track our progress, especially when editing a work or marketing a book. How do you know when you're "done?" Maintaining a to-do list saves you from working until you drop and feeling like you've still accomplished very little. For instance, when I market a book, I am careful to make lists such as, "Email reviewers" a task on my list that I do for a period of time and then cross off. I may email a set number of reviewers for several days, but unless I list it and cross it off, I'll either avoid doing it or fail to appreciate the time I've invested in it.

Besides keeping your work space relatively clear and cultivating a few organizational and writing habits to keep up with your work, set up a few monthly reminders in your calendar to follow up on several key areas for your work. For instance, a monthly scan of your website may reveal that you need to update your About page or swap out some items in your sidebar and footer. If I've written a new book, I need to consider how I plan to include it in my various online bio statements, such as Twitter, Facebook, and my website. If you're working as a freelancer, set a time each month to follow up with prospective clients who have either gotten in touch in the past or who could be a source of work in the future. If you're hoping to expand your writing network, set a time to subscribe to and read through a set number of blogs for 30-60 minutes.

Each month I make a habit of downloading the email addresses of readers who have downloaded my books on NoiseTrade. I generally use a specially designed email template that welcomes them to my list, suggests a few ways to keep in touch, and then offers them a book or two at a discounted price as a thank you for giving my work a shot. If I didn't set up a reminder and create a simple template to use for my first email to these new readers, I can't imagine I'd ever find a time to get around to it. Taking the time to set up a system with a reminder in my calendar has now become part of my monthly routine.

I know many authors who do a lot more than myself to maintain their writing careers. Many authors run split tests on two versions of their newsletters or websites to see which performs better. Others use statistics in programs such as Hootsuite to track their effectiveness on social media. Amazon's Associates program lets you track clicks on the links to books and other products you add to your website. I don't mess with most of that stuff. I generally try to pay attention to the titles of my blog posts and newsletters, but I don't get involved in tracking much beyond that. I'm sure people with a marketing background are shaking their heads with that one!

Besides keeping up with your website and reaching out to new clients or readers, your soul also needs special care throughout each day. In fact, if you're a Christian, I would argue that this is the most important aspect of personal maintenance. The notion of a sacred and secular divide can be especially harmful here. Our souls can be dragged down by our work, and therefore we need to both set aside time to care for our souls while also avoiding perspectives and practices in our work that can be damaging.

You will lose sight of your soul if you don't create space each day for God to speak and move. That may not sound like a big deal if you haven't invested too much time in sorting out what your soul is or what it feels like to have a soul that receives regular care. While I could say a lot about this, the most important aspect here is that your sense of worth and identity arises from your soul. Do you know that you are beloved and sought by God, or are you seeking acceptance from others? Are you writing out of the security of this acceptance or are you constantly tempted to perform for others or to adopt a false identity in order to win acceptance or fame? If we don't take time to re-center our souls, we'll soon drift in unhealthy directions.

While we can pray throughout our days and even remain aware of God while completing our work, dedicated time to rest in God's presence can serve to reorient us and allow God time to renew our minds. Rather than thinking of prayer as something you check off your list, think of it as something that you focus on for a specific period of time in order to move forward with the right mindset. Once you click into the right mindset, you can carry it with you throughout your day. To use another metaphor, it's a flame that you must tend to if you want it keep burning throughout the day when so many outside forces could snuff it out.

Personal Restoration

When I practice the Examen each evening, two important trends have emerged: I always look back at time spent reading or gardening as the most energizing parts of my days. While my wife and children are the greatest sources of my joy and contentment, I experience the most personal restoration when I take some quiet moments to myself each day. Since we've had young children for a few years now, that time could only last five or ten minutes, but I'm always better for it, even in limited quantities. Best yet, it's not uncommon for our family to garden together for at least part of the time that I'm working outside, so these practices don't always have to be solitary acts.

Setting aside time for my family, time by myself, and time to pray has become critically important for sustaining my writing work. No matter how significant my work may be at times, it's a poor substitute for my identity before God, the relationships with my family, and my personal health. Sometimes we fall into the trap of believing that we'll find personal fulfillment by throwing ourselves into a job that we'll love. In fact, the lure of a "dream job" could even lead to justifying an unhealthy obsession with our work. While freelance writing or book publishing could provide a much more satisfying and flexible career for many, it's certainly no substitute for the fulfillment that comes from cultivating a healthy prayer life, family life, and interior life.

I have thrown myself into my work for a season, and I can personally attest that it can't provide the fulfillment, joy, and restoration that we need. The deeper needs of our souls will eventually catch our attention one way or the other. The most important investments we make will be the ones that last in the Kingdom of God and in others. Writing can quickly turn into a way of storing up treasure for ourselves on earth. While we can mitigate that to a certain degree by using our writing for ministry, once that ministry gets tangled up with our finances, our priorities can slip out of focus quickly. In fact, if we know anything about people in full time ministry, it's that their souls can whither, burn out can knock them out, and their families can be neglected. Once you've devoted yourself to a big, important cause, such as writing about the Gospel or writing to meet an important need, you'll have all the more temptation to lose sight of your own soul and your family.

Sustainable writing means we set clear goals, work hard, and observe boundaries so that these essential aspects of our lives can flourish. I'll be the first to say that every writer needs to put in some serious hours and make a bunch of sacrifices in order to be productive and effective. I don't watch much television and had to really cut back on listening to podcasts. When we talked about places to live, one of the factors in our decision was finding a place we could rent that would be relatively low maintenance-- especially with a small lawn to mow. Writing professionally and sustainably should force us to make some tough decisions and sacrifices, but those sacrifices shouldn't extend to our families and spiritual lives. If anything, a healthy spiritual life has been extremely important in my productivity as a writer. If I'm ever feeling stuck on a writing project, the solution isn't necessarily to work into the evening. I typically need some time to rest, collect my thoughts, read a book, or just let my mind wander.

Whether you've been writing for years or you're just starting out, I want to encourage you to simplify your writing work as much as possible right now. If you're hoping to develop a fulfilling and sustainable career centered around your passions and talents, find the place where your interests and personal calling converge with what you can feasibly do right now for an income--even if you still need a day job for a season. You may only have the capacity to write in short spurts every day or you may have a few hours each day to devote to your writing work. Perhaps you can begin with weekly blog posts or e-newsletters. Perhaps you can just start writing books and use a short eBook download on your website to connect with readers. Then again, if you want to start building a freelancing business, you can start reading the best blogs in your field for tips and seek some pro bono clients to build a solid base of reviews for your website. There isn't necessarily a wrong way to move forward, so long as you're moving forward at a pace that is sustainable and leaves time to maintain your soul and the most important relationships in your life.

CHAPTER 8

PRIORITIES FOR SUSTAINABLE WRITING

What You Shouldn't Care about

I thought I had a clear calling from God to become a writer. I'm certain that I was right about that in a general sense. I also confused certain goals and desires with the pursuit of that calling--as if specific accomplishments were the only ways to validate that calling. It's true that every time I write, I feel like I'm moving in my own true north, but the path toward writing full time is paved with obstacles and compromises that left me frustrated and confused.

I'm still a work in progress here, but based on my observations of myself and my observations of others, here's how I've found a sustainable way forward--at least for now. In order to write sustainably, you need to relentlessly be yourself. That isn't necessarily the same thing as following a calling or your dreams. The difference is essential, in fact.

The writers who lead the most sustainable careers, at least in my circles, are the ones who recognize how they're wired and have a sense of how God has gifted them. They know what kind of writing is their own true north, but they also recognize when they need to take on work in order to make ends meet. They also have a clear sense of what drains them and what their limits are. One friend of mine makes a living through writing his own books and writing family histories for people who want to preserve their stories for generations to come. In order to market his own books, he had built a respectable social media presence, but over time, he felt how personally draining it was to keep up with the tweets and status updates. He regularly takes long sabbaticals from his social media accounts because they drained him emotionally, spiritually, and personally.

For me, I found tremendous freedom when I started publishing independently and didn't need to gather endorsements or line up a massive number of publicity opportunities for a book release. I still make a push of sorts to release my books, but it's nothing even close to what I've done when publishing commercially. I can spread out asking for favors, avoid the publicity I dislike, and spend the bulk of my time on writing. I can build my network and connections at my own pace without the threat of poor sales destroying my career. If anything, I regret waiting so long to jump into independent publishing with both feet because I have almost immediately mitigated nearly everything I dislike about commercial publishing. Mind you, I'm still open to publishing commercially, but I'm now committed to simply writing without getting derailed over the details of how it's published.

All caveats about the work you need to do in order to make a living aside, the faster you arrive at the point where you commit to just doing the kind of writing that gives you life and stop measuring every single metric, the better for you and your soul. That isn't to say that some entrepreneurial people will dive into analytics, SEO, and split testing for their work. I'm not out to condemn anyone. I've just seen how so many people who get life from writing are told by these analytics people to get cracking on their analytics and SEO and whatever else, and the writers fall to pieces under that pressure.

If you can make a book title or website more search engine-friendly or improve the keywords you use, there's no doubt that these things can help you become more successful. You could also double the number of hours you work and become more successful, but that doesn't mean you should. You won't find your own sweet spot for writing, freelancing, or publicity without some testing, risk, and limitations. For instance, I wanted to see how my independent book *Pray, Write, Grow* would do without endorsements from popular authors. I'm sure I could have asked a few authors who would have helped, but I personally don't put a lot of stock in endorsements these days. I focused on providing the book to reviewers in order to get feedback and early reviews. I can't tell you if it would have performed better if a few well-known authors had skimmed my introduction and written endorsements, but it did well enough without them. Depending on the project, I know that I can make it work without endorsers, saving myself from a process that I personally find draining and uncomfortable since it adds a commercial element to friendships and relationships with colleagues.

Removing myself from the endorsement game (or at least making it optional) has also provided the added benefit of releasing me from the influencer connection game. I know several influential authors who are regularly asked to endorse books, and more often than not, they dread it. One isn't even sure who wants to genuinely connect as a friend/colleague and who wants to leverage any kind of friendship for an endorsement.

Perhaps I'm especially sensitive these days to earn my book sales on my own merits rather than playing the endorsement connection game. Regardless of my reasons, I have felt more like myself without pursuing endorsements, and that helps me jump into a new day of writing with both feet. That doesn't mean that you shouldn't pursue endorsements for your books or that I won't pursue some endorsements in the future. Rather, assigning a lesser role to endorsements in my publishing career has made my work more sustainable and enjoyable. If you can name the two or three tasks that make your writing work miserable or dispiriting, why not look into some ways to eliminate them, outsource them, or mitigate their impact? That will free you to focus on what you care about the most when you start writing.

Finding Your Place as a Writer

Throughout this book I've been speaking to two very different situations even if many writers live in both: the writer who simply needs to earn a living and the writer who writes for more creative and artistic goals. The fortunate ones sometimes manage to merge the two together. Even then, the commercial success of one's writing can also introduce a whole new set of headaches. I assure you there will be moments when you'll reach tons of new readers and at a certain point you'll think to yourself: Who ARE these people? Thankfully, the vast majority of readers are very kind, and even the trolls are often hurting people who need a good friend or a more constructive hobby.

If you can write and make a living at it, by all means, go for it. However, if you're trying to publish books or build a blog that offer some sense of purpose and personal meaning, your sustainability and sanity will certainly hinge on finding topics that you care about and find personally fulfilling. The word sustainable doesn't mean we're talking about maximizing our profits, reaching the most readers, or winning all of the awards. We're talking about something that offers a measure of fulfillment, a respectable wage, and the potential to balance one's work and personal life. Experiment, take risks, and cut out what drains you if you can.

While some writers have found a way to make a comfortable living from their work, the majority of us will find that writing is far from the most profitable career option. However, income levels aren't quite as important as feeling like I'm finally doing what I was made to do. I spent most of my teen years and early 20's feeling completely unemployable--much as Anne Lamott describes herself in *Bird by Bird*. I honestly don't know what kind of job I would look for in the classified section if I gave up on writing today! If anything, that is an excellent motivator. My own career viability aside, very few people get into writing in order to strike it rich. OK, I did hear about this one lady who wrote a fad diet book, marketed it to the hilt, and then cashed in, but that's far from the norm. The rest of us start writing because we have a condition, an itch that we can only relieve by putting it into words.

I have writing ideas jotted down on post it notes, in my journal, on my computer, on my tablet, and on my phone. If I don't have a bit of paper and something to write with, I get nervous. While I could just do the bare minimum to earn a living by freelancing, I can't stop myself from blogging, writing books, and scribbling down one more idea. Writing is work, but it's also a source of life. The type of writing that gives life is often the most difficult work because I care about it so deeply. Editing is a true labor of love, and there is a ton of labor and love every day.

I've stopped asking whether I'm making enough sales, earning enough money, achieving enough success, or any other benchmark. You can drive yourself crazy and kill the joy of writing if you require a certain level of success. Pursuing it can leave you drained, stressed, and even bitter. Writing what you love and offering it as a gift removes you from the roller coaster of emotions. This combined with writing from a sense of security in God are the only ways I've been shielded from more toxic elements of writing.

Stop scrolling through Facebook and Twitter, envying what everyone else is doing. Stop comparing your website traffic, social media followers, sales rank, and income level.

Take a walk, go out for a coffee, or turn off every single electronic device in your home so you can journal in peace. If you're writing on your computer, use a program like Freedom or Self Control to cut yourself off from the noise of the world for a stretch of time. Sit in the quietest room you can find, and wait on the Holy Spirit. Hold onto a piece of scripture from today's Divine Hours and see where it leads you. Create space in your life for ideas to develop.

You are free to write. This isn't a race. We can only play our roles. Seek out what God has for you, give yourself to it, and let go of whatever success you see in others.

Early in my own career, I was deeply impacted by the following story about John the Baptist:

> An argument developed between some of John's disciples and a certain Jew over the matter of ceremonial washing. They came to John and said to him, "Rabbi, that man who was with you on the other side of the

Jordan--the one you testified about--look, he is baptizing, and everyone is going to him."

To this John replied, "A person can receive only what is given them from heaven. You yourselves can testify that I said, 'I am not the Messiah but am sent ahead of him.' The bride belongs to the bridegroom. The friend who attends the bridegroom waits and listens for him, and is full of joy when he hears the bridegroom's voice. That joy is mine, and it is now complete. He must become greater; I must become less."

John 3:25-30, NIV

We all have our parts to play, but we'll only find contentment if we invest in seeking our own roles and joyfully carrying them out. John the Baptist had a slight advantage since a FREAKING ANGEL appeared to his father in order to announce his life's purpose. Still, John deserves credit for jumping into his calling with both feet. He moved out into the dessert and played his part as a prophet, even dressing like Elijah. He didn't begrudge the audiences who sought out Jesus because he saw himself as the messenger and nothing more. We can only point people in the right direction. We all have our limits. If anything, limits help us thrive and achieve contentment because we can see the blessings we can experience and share where we are right now. I mean, if you want to spend your life pining away for another role or more success, be my guest. I've tried it, and it didn't suit me.

We hear advice all of the time like this:

Do what you love.

Do what you're passionate about.

Follow your dream.

Pursue conflict and live a good story

This advice isn't necessarily wrong. It's just incomplete

without the insight John the Baptist offers. Our passions, dreams, and loves can be so very important in guiding us toward work that could be meaningful for us and for others, but the direction we receive from God comes before everything else. If we know our roles and embrace them with all of our love and passion, then we'll have something significant to offer. The joy of writing will become a reward all its own.

Sustainable writing means using our unique gifts and experiences to write in ways that reflect where God is leading us and what God is calling us to do. If you love telling stories, continue to nurture that part of you that loves to tell a good tale. If you love explaining how things work, find the technical writing field that leaves you fascinated and engaged. If you want to share out of your own experiences or research, start writing the books or articles that are already rolling around in your head as shapeless ideas. Sustainability means you can keep writing for the long haul even after receiving bad news from an editor, failing to land a client, or making a huge mistake on your website. If you're truly drawn to something and you know your role in the grand scheme of things, how can you stop yourself, let alone let anyone stop you?

What has God given you to share?

If you start to share that, you may never stop writing.

Thank You for Reading!

You're Invited to Join My Community of Readers

You can get TWO FREE eBooks, first dibs (as well as discounts) on new book releases, and learn about my other books by signing up for my e-newsletter.

Sign up at www.edcyzewski.com

I also post weekly at www.edcyzewski.com about writing and prayer, and I spend a bit of time each day on Facebook and Twitter. I'd love it if you dropped by to say hello.

What Did You Think of *Write without Crushing Your Soul*?

Can you take a moment to leave a brief review at a major reading site like Amazon or Goodreads? Your review will help readers know if they should give this book a shot, and I'd be grateful if you took a few minutes to do this!

AFTERWORD

This book took shape after a series of conversations with writing colleagues brought up a single surprise that all of our careers had in common: pain. Writing for a living brings on pain in shapes and quantities that we never could have predicted. That doesn't mean they regretted their careers or the work they had done. The problem is that writers are often working in solitude, and it doesn't feel right to spend our limited social time together talking about our disappointments, failures, and struggles. Who wants to be the one to kick off THAT conversation?

Since that conversation never materialized until long after we had all plunged into writing books and freelancing, we were all caught by surprise. It's my hope that *Write without Crushing Your Soul* is more than a guide to a sustainable writing career. I hope that the readers of this book feel a new freedom to have frank conversations about their careers, whether that's a particular struggle or failure. We need to recognize that every writer is in the midst of an epic battle to do the work of writing while keeping their souls in a healthy place.

At the very least, you can get together with your friends and laugh about how you're not as bad off as that "Ed what's-his-name guy" (If you're wondering, my name is pronounced Cy-zes-key, which is Americanized Polish and is very confusing for everyone).

Writing is going to hurt, but you can handle it.

There are many threats to the health of your soul, but it's worth protecting.

Rejection and failure are certainly coming, but there is an endless well of peace and joy found in the acceptance that God offers us.

For what it's worth, there's a guy out there who has seen a bit of the ups and downs of the writing business, and he is cheering for you to succeed. He cares about your health and sustainability as a writer so much that he wrote over 60,000 words that he's hoping will save you from the worst things that could happen. We're all in this together, and we're only going to make it if we all help each other out-- even the good people who write Amish vampire romance novels.

Other Books by Ed Cyzewski

Books for Writers

- Pray, Write, Grow: Cultivating Prayer and Writing Together
- Creating Space: The Case for Everyday Creativity
- A Path to Publishing: What I Learned by Publishing a Nonfiction Book

Christian Living Books

- A Christian Survival Guide: A Lifeline to Faith and Growth
- Why We Run from God's Love
- Unfollowers: Unlikely Lessons on Faith from Those Who Doubted Jesus
- The Good News of Revelation
- Hazardous: Committing to the Cost of Following Jesus
- Divided We Unite: Practical Christian Unity
- Coffeehouse Theology: Reflecting on God in Everyday Life

Visit Ed's blog for samples and ordering info:

http://edcyzewski.com/my-books/

Pick Up Discounted eBooks here:

http://edcyzewski.com/writing-and-christianity-e-books

Pray, Write, Grow: Cultivating Prayer and Writing Together

If you want to improve your prayer life, try writing.
If you want to improve your writing life, try praying.

The two require many of the same practices, disciplines, and virtues. If you're already inclined to both write and pray, you may as well figure out how they can help each other. If you're experienced in one, you may find opportunities for personal or spiritual growth by trying out the other.

This book offers life-giving practices that will help you grow in both prayer and writing and show how the two can work together to improve your craft as a writer and your spiritual practices as a person of faith

A Path to Publishing: What I Learned by Publishing a Nonfiction Book
(2014, Revised Edition)

A Path to Publishing is a big-picture, step-by-step guide for nonfiction publishing hopefuls. Beginning with mental preparation for writing and building a platform, Cyzewski helps readers develop their ideas, write regularly, pitch a proposal, and market their work. Through accounts of his experiences, a series of case studies, and action steps, each chapter moves readers toward the final goal of becoming published writers.

Creating Space: The Case for Everyday Creativity

Creativity is a gift everyone has been given to share, but doubt, discouragement, and distractions hinder the ability of many to pursue their creative passions. *Creating Space* advocates for the creative gifts in every person, arguing that...

- Creativity is not a mistake.
- Creativity can be developed.
- Creativity is a vitally important gift for others.

This brief manifesto on creativity is for everyone. Whether you doodle, sing in the shower, knit scarves, or scribble poems, *Creating Space* will encourage you to make space in your life in order to fulfill your creative calling, using your gifts to their fullest extent.

Unfollowers: Unlikely Lessons on Faith from Those Who Doubted Jesus

Ed Cyzewski and Derek Cooper

Unfollowers re-tells the Gospels from the perspectives of those who ignored or opposed Jesus, asking the question: What can followers of Jesus learn from the dropouts, detractors, and doubters of the Gospels? Their stories guide us in overcoming common obstacles to discipleship and remind us that following Jesus is often counter-intuitive and surprising.

The Good News of Revelation

Ed Cyzewski and Larry Helyer

The original readers of Revelation had a very different experience of John's letter compared to the fear and anxiety that grips readers today. John intended his letter to encourage seven suffering churches to persevere as they waited for Christ's return. Rather than detailing a rapture that escapes suffering, Revelation has a message about suffering, good vs. evil, and the justice of God that is relevant for John's audience and readers today.

A Christian Survival Guide: A Lifeline to Faith and Growth

A Christian Survival Guide uses humor and straightforward, biblical answers to help life-long Christians and new believers grow in their relationships with God by tackling the tough questions and common pitfalls in Christian belief and practice. Rather than permitting persistent sin and lingering doubts to hold them back from God, Christians can shore up their faith by getting the basics of Christianity straight, and moving into a thriving relationship with God, even if every question isn't answered. Readers will be encouraged to run the race of faith in order to win--albeit with a cramp from a good laugh.

Coffeehouse Theology: Reflecting on God in Everyday Life

Coffeehouse Theology will help readers understand, shape, and live out their beliefs. Beginning with a discussion about the ways cultural context impacts theology, *Coffeehouse Theology* roots theology in the church's mission to be the presence of God's Kingdom. Far from dividing the church, theology unites the church in a dynamic dialogue about the presence of God, his revelation in scripture, and the interpretations of the historic and global churches.

Hazardous: Committing to the Cost of Following Jesus
Ed Cyzewski and Derek Cooper

Hazardous encourages disciples of Jesus to count the steep costs of following Jesus in their daily lives by equipping them to pursue holiness, listen for God's guidance, and obey God's direction. A lot of books tell us that discipleship is costly, but this book shows what it looks like and how God helps us persevere in the midst of trials.

For more info, visit: <u>http://edcyzewski.com/my-books</u>

ABOUT THE AUTHOR

Ed Cyzewski writes at www.edcyzewski.com where his love for prayer, writing, and bad puns come together. He is the author of *Pray, Write Grow: Cultivating Prayer and Writing Together* (a bestseller), *Coffeehouse Theology, A Christian Survival Guide,* and other books. He is a graduate of Biblical Theological Seminary, avid gardener, hockey fan, and devotee to New York style pizza.

Find him on twitter: @edcyzewski and on http://www.facebook.com/EdCyzewskiWriter. Subscribe to his e-newsletter for new book releases, discounts, and tips on writing and publishing.